'Only he who attempts the absurd
is capable of achieving the impossible'

FRED HASLAM, champion rabbit breeder

'Every man over forty is
responsible for his own face'

ABRAHAM LINCOLN

Roger Law

A Nasty Piece of Work

**With Lewis Chester
and Alex Evans**

Photograph: David King

Dedicated to my mother and father

Editor: Edward Booth-Clibborn

Collaborative writer: Lewis Chester

Book designer: Alex Evans

Editorial co-ordinator: Lesley Baxter

Research: Peter Jones

Set in Garamond, Gill Sans and Block Condensed

Text output by: Letter Space
Red Lion Court, Hounslow, Middlesex

Printed by: Jolly & Barber
Hillmorton Road, Rugby, Warwickshire

Published by: Booth-Clibborn Editions
18, Colville Road, London W3 8BL

Distributed by: Internos Books
18, Colville Road, London W3 8BL
World publishing rights reserved
ISBN 1873 968 000

Picture frame on front cover kindly supplied by:
Paul Mitchell, New Bond Street, London W1

Contents

Growing up in Littleport, in the heart of the Fens, my first artistic inspiration was Mr Baumber, the sign-writer. The impressive thing about Mr Baumber was not so much the excellence of his signs but the casual elegance of his way of life. Unlike my father and my uncles, he seemed to exist very much on his own terms. The little work that he did he seemed to enjoy, and for the rest of the time he would be pleasantly inebriated. You could say, in modern psychological terms, that he was my first serious role model.

Fen Tiger

Photograph: Peter Keen

ven Mr Baumber's imperfections had charm. It was said that his one serious deficiency as a sign-writer was a tendency to spell in a highly individual way. Thus when he painted the sign for my father's building business, Law Brothers Building Constructors, his version came out "Law Brothers Building Constrictors". I later came to feel that Mr Baumber may have grasped an essential truth about the enterprise.

In the modern era of second homes and high-speed motorways, it is hard to imagine just how cut off from the rest of the world the Fens seemed in those days. My father would tell me about the time he had taken his workforce up to London to see the sights. This was reckoned a great success by the men, who spent the whole day going up and down the escalators at Liverpool Street Station. The only improbability about this story to me as a child was the idea of my father ever allowing his workers off site for a whole day.

I was a wartime baby, born on 6 September 1941, but I cannot say that I knew much of the war's privations. Living close to the land we never went short of fresh eggs and vegetables. My father was away in the army but, by all accounts, he spent more of his time fighting his own officers than he did fighting Hitler. A high proportion of his military service was spent in the glass house. My only graphic memory of the period was of a huge effigy of Hitler being burned in the centre of Littleport. I thought that was really impressive.

Even as a child in the Fens you had the sense of living on the edge. There was always the feeling that the water might one day reclaim the land and that Littleport, a landlocked little town-cum-village of some 4,000 inhabitants on the border between Norfolk and Cambridgeshire, might easily revert to its island status. As kids we would go out with our poles to certain fields and poke the apparent solid surface of the earth. Three or four feet down it would be like jelly. And if the place did not sink without trace, there seemed a good chance of its being blown away by the icy winds that came howling across the open spaces, straight from Siberia.

The character of the people was less wintry than the terrain, but it was to some extent shaped by it. Since the earliest times the Fen country has been a natural refuge for outlaws, as the bogs deterred hot pursuit by the forces of law and order. Hereward the Wake held out against the Norman invaders in the marshes round Ely before he was betrayed by a greedy abbot. In Regency times the Fens were a popular hideout for runaway black slaves, which accounts for some of today's more exotic physiognomies.

The inaccessibility of the area was also prized by its more law-abiding inhabitants. When they started to drain the Fens, there was no end to the problems with the local labour hired to do the work. They would dig the

trenches for money by day, and fill them in at night for free. They were the original Fen Tigers. Eventually they brought in Irish navvies.

The works of central government were regarded with distrust, sometimes with good reason. It was a rising in Littleport that sparked the riots round the country in the wake of the Napoleonic Wars. These were stamped out with great ferocity and in 1816 five men of Littleport were hanged for their part in the rioting. I was well acquainted with many of their descendants.

A sense of being at odds with the world beyond the Fens, even though many people made a living by selling produce to it, was very much a part of my growing up. One consequence of this peculiar solidarity was that there was not a lot of class feeling, though some were richer than others. Nor was there much in the way of professional arrogance. The ranks of Fenland doctors and dentists contained an unusually large number of people who had been chucked out of the Royal Navy.

Left: my parents, George Law and Winifred Hiblin in their courting days, 1939.
Above: my grandfather, Robert Law, judging horseflesh at Ely cattle market, *circa* **1925**
Overleaf: Fen country
Photograph: Alain Blaire

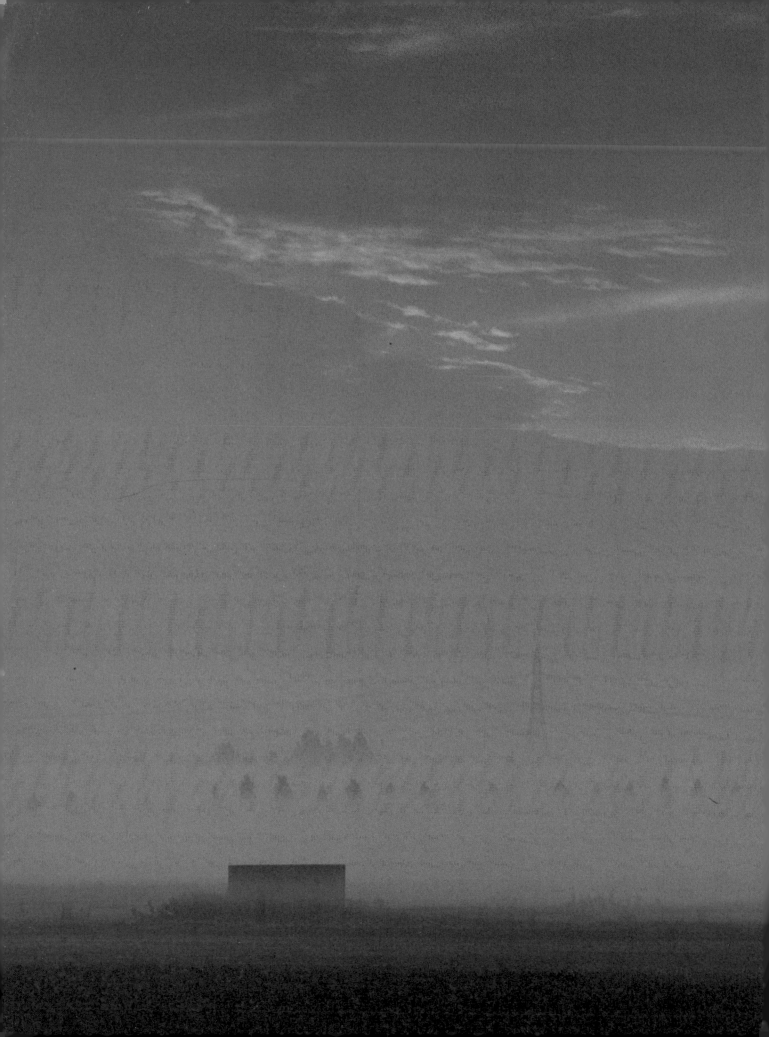

y own family's tradition was essentially muscular. My grandfather Robert, who died when my own father was eight years old, was a revered figure. He had originally been a blacksmith before making a great success as a general dealer. He invested all his money in cattle and prospered to the extent of opening a couple of butcher's shops in the village and even sold his meat pies in London. His business was then completely wiped out by a foot and mouth epidemic. Soon after, he died a typical Fenland death. A horse and carriage crashed through the ice on the Wash and my grandfather helped rescue the trapped driver. He then went home and died of pneumonia.

He had thirteen children, eleven surviving, and these were farmed out among different families in Littleport, which gave me a tremendous range of aunts and uncles as a child. The Laws were rather a stoic breed, without being dour, and also quite ambitious, none more so than my father.

My father, I often felt, was a driven man, and the drive was to restore the fortune that Fate had so cruelly wrested from the grasp of his own father. At various times he had three other brothers, Bill, Jack and Felix, working with him in the construction business, which hugely profited from the postwar council housing boom in the Fens. But there were absolutely no family favours. The workers were expected to work at the double but George Law's nearest and dearest relations were expected to die for the business.

The more cosmopolitan side of my upbringing came from my mother, Winifred, and her family, the Hiblins. My mother's parents ran the dairy in Littleport but they were acquainted with a wider world. They had run a shop in the East End of London and my grandmother Jenny had worked in Birmingham for many years, in a supervisory capacity in the rag trade. She knew all the old music hall songs and was a lot of fun, if a bit sharp with it. Her husband was more subdued, but not unimpressive. Wilfrid Hiblin had served in World War One, and had lived to tell the tale, though with some difficulty. While on ambulance duty on the front line, part of his jaw had been shot away.

My grandparents were also remarkable for being among the first people in the neighbourhood to own a television set, and I can remember, aged twelve, being forced for hours to watch a snowstorm on it called "The Coronation" when I wanted to be out playing. This undoubtedly damaged any royalist tendencies I might have had.

There was an unspoken but implicit assumption among the Hiblins that my mother, who had been to grammar school in Ely, had married slightly beneath her. Apparently my father had wooed and won her by clambering over seven rows of seats in the Empire cinema, Littleport, to be by her side.

Politically, the Hiblins were quite sophisticated and refined, being of the Liberal persuasion.

My father's political outlook is something I still find hard to define. From the frequency with which he said a problem could be solved by shooting somebody, you might think he was a Fascist. At the same time he had nothing but contempt for what might be described as the professional shooting classes, like the army for example. His firmest belief was in work and it would be hard to find a more instinctive capitalist, or a man more totally wedded to the proposition that people should rise by their own bootstraps. Yet when the Tories were in power they would be denigrated as "Them" as opposed to "Us". Like many people in the Fens, he was fiercely anti-authority while being quite a considerable authority figure himself. While I was growing up he always voted Labour, but he would have a late-flowering love affair with the politics of Mrs Thatcher.

I probably learned more trying to figure out where my father was coming from than I ever did from school, where I was mainly distinguished for my misbehaviour. After acquiring the rudiments of the 3Rs, education in the Fens did not seem to lead anywhere much. In those days there were eight grammar school places reserved for eleven-plus successes in the whole of the Isle of Ely. There did not seem much point in trying, particularly when Littleport Secondary Modern had the reputation for being a good laugh.

When I first went there the headmaster's favourite activity was playing the violin to an accompaniment of Fenland birdsong whistled by the boys. Unfortunately, he left to be replaced by a Mr Browning, who had the much more ridiculous notion of turning the enterprise into a mini public school with houses, prefects and all that nonsense. I could not take to it, so I became disruptive. I would invite trouble by saying "Hello" instead of "Yes Sir" when the register was being called, and I would be caned for each offence until the form master got bored with hitting me. One new master marked our first encounter by belting me across the room and saying, "Now Law, you can do one thing wrong." My reputation had evidently preceded me, and he was getting his retaliation in first.

My real education was in the holidays when, as the elder son, I was expected to immerse myself in the ways of the family business. And that meant working with my father and his brothers on the building sites, where health and safety regulations were honoured only in the breach.

On a Law Brothers', more popularly known as "Claw Brothers'", site everything was done on piece rates at breakneck speed, and if there was a corner to be cut my father would cut it. It was said of him that he did not lay bricks down so much as "throw them down". We would recycle track from disused railways lines, doors from old Nissen huts, anything that could be scavenged. We used wooden scaffolding, long past its day, and our holes would be left routinely and dangerously unsupported. The firm had acquired a reputation as the

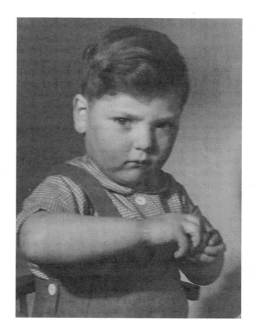

Roger Law, *circa* **1942.**

fastest contract builders in the East and my father aimed to keep it, whatever the building regulations might say. All this frantic activity would be laced with George Law's special line in inspirational messages for the workers, all variants on, "If the dog hadn't stopped for a crap he'd have caught the hare."

If the building inspector came by asking who was the governor, we were all trained to say, "We're all the boss here." I remember one inspector, more tenacious than most, managed to figure out that the man up aloft bricking the chimney was the boss. So he took off after my father, shinning up one of our typical ramshackle structures and caused the whole thing to collapse. He fell and broke both ankles, while my father stayed aloft, secure with his chimney.

One day Uncle Bill had a heart attack on the roof. We had two pulleys, one of which worked fine, the other of which was known to be dodgy. As we were preparing to lower him with the good mechanism, Uncle Jack's voice floated up from below: "Don't put him on there, boys. We're bringing the bricks up." So the sick man, fortunately without mishap, went down on the dodgy pulley.

Experiences of this kind began to concentrate my young mind. By the age of thirteen I had become acquainted with most of the trials and terrors of a construction worker's life. I had worked incredibly long hours - close of business on a Law Brothers' site would be heralded by Uncle Jack standing on top of a gable end and shouting for one last push: "The day is short, and the night is long, so get along my old beauties." I had enjoyed the experience of having my hands stuck fast by the hoar frost to scaffolding clamps, and having to prize them off with warm tea. I had staggered under the weight of a concrete lintel and all but gone over the edge of the scaffolding. My Uncle Jack grabbed me and saved me, without saying a word. I got the impression that this was business as usual, so I went down and got another lintel.

Very occasionally I would mention to my father that the work did seem rather hard, but this would only lead to an early version of the Monty Python sketch in which the participants brag competitively about the awfulness of their origins. Whatever I might have suffered, he had suffered ten times worse. At the same time, he was not an unkind man. He did not, for example, think I should go into the world defenceless. Sometimes, without my mother's knowledge, we would sneak off to Chatteris where there was a boxing club, made famous by Eric Boon, where I was shown the ropes and introduced to the Noble Art.

Despite this compensation, a powerful conviction was forming in my mind that fulfilling my father's expectations of me was just about the last thing I wanted to do on leaving school. The future leadership of the Law Brothers' Construction empire would, I felt, be much better entrusted to my young brother Martin. But the way out for me was not immediately apparent.

I had always liked to draw but there did not seem to be much scope for

earning an artistic living in Littleport, other than in the sign-writing area which Mr Baumber had cornered. I had always drawn for fun rather than as a career prospect, though it had brought me some local notoriety. On Feast Days - the main public holiday of the year for the farming community - people would come from all around to show off their horses and vegetables in Littleport. And there would be little competition tents where people could demonstrate their prowess. I would show a few rabbits and some drawings, which would invariably win first or second prize. One of my more ambitious designs was a large crayon portrait of Clem Attlee, done on a hoarding, which helped Labour to lose the 1951 Election.

It was my mother who first grasped that my backwardness at school need be no deterrent to further education, which she evidently thought I required. In those days, though not alas now, you could gain admittance to an art school solely on the strength of your art work without any formal qualifications. Accordingly, I submitted a slim portfolio of my Feast Day studies to the Cambridge School of Art and was, to my great surprise, accepted.

I was not unhappy to take my leave of Littleport Secondary Modern, and the pleasure, it seemed, was wholly mutual. Mr Browning's last headmasterly words to me were:"I don't know what will happen to you in life but wherever you go I hope you will learn some manners."

Left: as Long John Silver, aged nine, with my jackdaw.
Above: family reunion, 1950. My parents, second and third from right in back row, some distance from their elder son, Roger, aged nine, with tongue out in front row.

When I first arrived at art school, still some days short of my fifteenth birthday, I really thought

that I had died and gone to heaven. I had half feared that it would be an extention of ordinary school, but there was no catch as far as I could see. Within weeks I was smoking as many Woodbines as I could lay my hands on and getting to gaze, through my studies in Life Class, at a variety of naked women. My spirit was in no way crushed by the discovery that Mr Baumber's expertise in sign-writing could only be approached through a narrow door, marked "Calligraphy". Since I had not yet managed the art of joined-up handwriting, I knew that my chances of proceeding very far in this direction were slim. But I did not mind in the least, as I could see so many other more exotic possibilities opening up before me.

Coming up Woodbines

Photograph: David King

In those broad-minded days, the preliminary to the commercial art course consisted of a Cook's tour of all the basic crafts - life and plant drawing, sculpting and modelling, painting, ceramics, woodcuts, stage design and calligraphy. Unlike the custom in the narrow, three-year graphic design courses of today, no running before walking was allowed. You had to have some grounding in all these areas before you were allowed to specialise. But then the course took four years, almost five in my case as some remedial effort was involved.

To compensate for the largely self-imposed inadequacies of my Littleport education, I was initially put on a course of general literary and historical studies run by a man called David Joseph, who subsequently rose to great heights in the Open University. I did not come to this discipline with a wholly virgin brain as my mind was brimful of Krazy Kat, L'il Abner, and numerous other American comics readily available in Littleport as surplus to the requirements of the surrounding US air bases like Mildenhall and Alconbury.

Joseph enriched the mixture with injections of Dylan Thomas, John Steinbeck, J.D. Salinger and John Osborne and, in the process, gave me an appetite for literature that I could never have acquired in the regimented atmosphere of my old school. The fact that there were no mandatory examinations may also have helped, though I did take an 'O' level paper in History and passed, thanks to a heaven-sent question on the Littleport riots.

The art school, originally founded by John Ruskin, was quite small, with only about 100 pupils who were taught in groups of ten or twelve. The technical college, of which it formed a part, was grafted on later and run on more sausage-machine lines. There were a number of Fenland potato-heads like myself on the technical side but the art school tended to exhibit a much wider social range. There were earnest grammar school types and a good sprinkling of public schoolboys whose company in the college, and in the university, I tended to prefer for its more irresponsible quality. We were also uplifted by the presence of some very upper-class girls with double-barrelled names, who had been sent to the Cambridge School of Art to find a husband, preferably from the university.

To the task of teaching this motley group, the staff brought an admirable attention to detail. Some of the older tutors had been taught anatomy at the Slade by Henry Tonks, a man of legendary application. During the First World War, Tonks had been asked about his feelings when he composed drawings of wounded soldiers on the front line. "It's a chamber of horrors," Tonks said, "but I am quite content to draw them as it is excellent practice."

In keeping with the Tonks tradition, we had to do drawings of absolutely gigantic plaster magnifications of human ears, feet and hands which, now that

I come to think about it, were much weirder than anything you might see on *Spitting Image*. Another arcane area was Basic Design, where the tutor would draw lines all over a painting showing how the dog's nose lined up with the table-mat. The commitment of all our tutors was impressive, though few could excel John Norris-Wood, who took us for natural history drawing and kept a crocodile in his bath.

During my first year in art school, I grew up very fast to well over six feet. As a result, I would be looking around for fellows of my own age who might make useful drinking companions without giving me a crick in the neck. One morning in Life Class, at the start of my second year, I spotted what looked like a suitable case. He was a tall, fair-haired new boy who was looking at the model with that peculiar tense expression which indicated that he was watching his first naked lady. I went up behind him and said, "Hello mate, I come from Littleport."

Peter Fluck was hardly my ideal as a friend. For one thing he was neither fellow potato-head nor a public schoolboy. He was the son of a grocer and, that despised breed, the grammar schoolboy, with four 'O' levels to prove it. We were almost exactly the same age but he had wasted the previous year at school amassing these impressive qualifications. The other galling thing about Fluck was that he was absolutely ace at lettering, with virtually no formal training. I used to ascribe this skill to the frequency with which he had to repaint the 'L' in the sign over his father's shop in Park Street.

I do not think I was Peter Fluck's ideal as a friend either. I think I was, and probably remained, a shade too boisterous and uncouth for his more refined taste. The thing that doomed us to each other's company was the fact that we made each other laugh.

Very shortly after our first meeting, we left the bosoms of our respective families and set up as independent men of the world in a shambolic room in a house on the Oxford Road. We would sleep there at opposite sides of a large double bed in chaste amity. Soon after this ménage had been established, I took up with Deirdre Amsden, who was among the more capable students in our class and the possessor of a most entrancing bum. The consequence was that Deirdre moved in and Fluck found himself forced out of the room onto a mattress in the hallway. Fortunately, he had to laugh.

Life at college was enjoyably disrupted by the arrival of Alec Heath who, as the new principal, rapidly started to introduce new men. The man brought in to ginger up the drawing was Paul Hogarth, a descendant of the original William Hogarth, though this was his least significant credential.

Unlike the men of the Tonks tradition, Hogarth was a really exciting character. He was not a career teacher but someone who lived by selling his skill in the marketplace and this, Fluck and I had decided, was very much the way we wanted to go. Hogarth also demonstrated the possibilities for combining art

Above: at art school, aged sixteen, deeply pondering an early clay model.
Left: Paul Hogarth in thoughtful attitude at a garden party.
Photograph: Roger Law

Brittany landscape, charcoal drawing by Roger Law, 1959.

with action. He had travelled the world, drawing and politicking when the occasion demanded. He had driven relief lorries in the Spanish Civil War, and later in Poland in the 1940s. In the early fifties, he had been among the first to open up Eastern Europe and China to Western eyes through his drawing. Though identified with Communist causes, his work was most celebrated in the United States, where it appeared regularly in magazines like *Fortune* and *Sports Illustrated*.

He was also appealing to us for the way he had mislaid his first wife. She had told him that if he worked with "yet another drunken writer" she would be on her way. As it happened, Hogarth had accepted a commission to do the illustrations for a book about Ireland, working in collaboration with Brenda Behan, one of the island's thirstiest inhabitants. The book was a great success, but it was the end of a marriage.

It was through Hogarth that we became acquainted with the concept of the "artist reporter", essentially the artist dealing with topical issues of the day as his raw material. This was immensely appealing as I was drawn to the idea of making visual statements rather than just representations. And I was already

dabbling in caricature.

This was not one of Hogarth's specialisms but, unlike his predecessors, he encouraged this form of expression. Indeed, he went so far as to publicise one of his own exhibitions with a caricature of himself done by me. This was a brave act considering that his hairstyle was not dissimilar to that of Bobby Charlton.

Hogarth's greatest gift to us was access to his library. Both Fluck and I were already well versed in the English tradition - Gillray, Cruikshank and the rest - but Hogarth had an enormous range of European stuff that we had never clapped eyes on. We would descend on his home at weekends and devour back issues of *L'Assiette au Beurre* (which colloquially translates as *Gravy Train*), the brainchild of Samuel Schwarz, a Polish Jew who made his original stake by selling soft-porn in French garrison towns. The best illustrations were to be found in the early twentieth-century numbers, where all the issues of the day - from concentration camps to the Dreyfus Affair - were confronted with fierce satirical energy. And Hogarth would show us books of drawings by George Grosz about Hitler's Germany in the thirties, which were so powerful they gave you the feeling of almost being there.

Roche Rock in Cornwall as a woodcut, my first tottering step in advertising, done for a Shell calendar in the early sixties.

Beside the seaside

The unofficial Cambridge School of Art agitprop team frolics by the Scarborough shore after an exhausting night at the 1960 Labour Party conference spent plastering the conference hotels with "Gaitskell Must Go" and "Ban the Bomb" posters. From left: Roger Law, Peter Fluck, Deirdre Amsden, Graham Ludford and Christopher Harrison.

LE CAPITALISME

Celui-là fait une guerre terrible, inexorable, chaque jour, à toutes les heures du jour. Mais ces messieurs de la Conférence ne s'en occuperont pas....

he most practical thing that Hogarth helped to provide was contacts. He got on to the university and told them there was no reason why their publications should look so execrable when there were so many able art students resident in the same town. Partly as a result, Deirdre and I got to art-edit a number of university organs, including six issues of *Granta*, a young thinking man's magazine if ever there was one. Our successor on *Granta* was Peter Fluck.

Our other contacts with the university were more informal. There was a girl in our class called Wendy Snowden who fell in love with, and later married, an undergraduate by the name of Peter Cook. So we all became friendly. Cook was a funny man but you would hardly have picked him as the father figure of the satire revolution that was then lurking just around the corner. To this he gave, among many imperishable lines - "not a million miles from the truth" and "my lady wife whose name escapes me". In appearance then he was like a Regency buck, but pleasantly diffident with it. If he had a keen interest, other than in the horse-racing pages of the national newspapers, I never noticed what it was. But he became a kind of benefactor.

Cook owned a building in Park Street a few doors down from Fluck's the grocers and it had some surplus space. He allowed Fluck, Deirdre and myself to occupy the ground floor and to put up a Fluck-fashioned sign announcing that East Anglian Artists was open for business. Since neither Fluck nor I was on a grant, we both came under a certain amount of parental pressure to earn a few bob. My father tended to treat me with all the reverence that he might accord to an out of work actor, though he could never quite bring himself to wish me out of college and into the army, an ever present possibility with conscription still in force.

East Anglian Artists, being on a flightpath to Cook, who lived upstairs, attracted some intriguing visitors. One was David Frost, though there was actually not a lot of point in knowing Frost if you already knew Cook because he would retell Cook's jokes, almost word for word. East Anglian Artists never did do much business. Nor, for that matter, did our movie. This was a delicate study of Deirdre and myself as two beautiful young people with Fluck brilliantly empathising the role of an imbecilic old man. Shot on location in a country home and in a scrap metal yard, it was taken to New York by its student director in search of a niche market. Neither he nor the film have ever been seen or heard of since.

Eventually Fluck and I discovered that we could make more serious money by doing the early morning cleaning at Fitzwilliam House and by waiting on table for the undergraduates at Trinity, where we became celebrated as the "Gypsy Menace". It was not therefore very long before self-service catering

Left: the French magazine, *L'Assiette au Beurre*, dealt in powerful images and big subjects as in this study of capitalism by Galantara, published early this century.
Top: *L'Assiette au Beurre*, a typical early 20th-century cover.
Below: woodcut print by Ed Middleditch, my print-making tutor at the Cambridge School of Art.
Photograph: Ron Stellitano

was introduced.

For all our reverses on the economic front, we were rarely idle. The late fifties were the early days for the peace movement, which reached its crescendo with the Aldermaston marches. Many of us were deeply involved in the Campaign for Nuclear Disarmament (CND), and its more militant wing, the Committee of 100. There were some staid figures in the college who thought this provided evidence of Hogarth leading the young astray, but this was not so. Hogarth by this time had left the Communist Party a disillusioned man. The one thing he never wanted to talk about was contemporary politics.

It is hard, looking back, to recapture the intensity and anger of that period. But I think it boiled down to a feeling that we had been hoodwinked about the nature and extent of the nuclear threat. When you stripped away all the reassuring rhetoric about nuclear war being "limited", you realised that meant limited to Britain and a few others who had drawn short straws in Europe. And no matter how limited any conflict managed to get, you could be sure that Littleport, with its friendly neighbourhood US bomber bases, would have no chance. Later generations would learn how to become more fatalistic about the nuclear threat but mine was idealistic, or perhaps innocent, enough to believe that things could be changed.

Blessed with a grandfather who was deeply versed in the horrors of war and who seemed only too delighted to pay my fines, I became a none-too-pacific peace agitator. My time spent being picked on in pubs as a serious underage drinker had equipped me well for the confrontational stuff to which every demonstration is prone, while my art school training was all I needed by way of entrance to the crude but exciting world of agitprop.

David Joseph, my literary mentor at college, had a friend called Richard Fletcher who paved the way. Fletcher was a very intriguing man who had invented a method for sticking aluminium filaments onto plastic and paper. You can see examples of its application in the average packet of peanuts. Unfortunately for Fletcher, he patented the machine that churned the stuff out rather than the process itself, and he missed out on a gold mine in royalties. Aside from being a distraught inventor, he was also a property developer, the publisher of a magazine called *Union Voice*, and a Labour Party fixer of a very high order. Fletcher was aiming to fix things so that the Labour Party would come out in favour of unilateral disarmament, which it did at the Scarborough conference in 1960, only to do a U-turn a year later.

Fluck and I and several other mates at college supplied the artistic shock effects for Fletcher's posters and pamphlets, indicting Hugh Gaitskell and the right-wing Labour leadership for all its revisionist works. Fletcher, in his turn, provided logistical support, in the form of a van. We would use this to travel to the big union and party conferences, where we would plaster the neighbourhood, with special reference to the delegate's bedroom and breakfast room

Ticket for an art school party, an early work.

The Cambridge Review

May Week Number

SATURDAY, JUNE 3, 1961   (REGISTERED AS A NEWSPAPER)   PRICE SIXPENCE

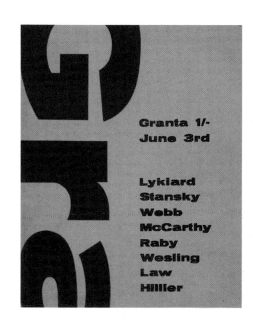

Granta 1/-
June 3rd

Lykiard
Stansky
Webb
McCarthy
Raby
Wesling
Law
Hillier

IN TEARS JEAN yCLITHON TVRNED FROM BURNING ATHENS! & STARTED TO MOUNT HELICON

ON THE WAY THEY MET PICASSO. MY FRIENDS! HE SAID ONE OF MY MODELS WILL TAKE YOU TO OEDIPVS REX

Work for Cambridge university publications. Top left: one of my covers for *Cambridge Review*. Right: a *Granta* cover by Deirdre Amsden. Below: a cartoon of mine for *Cambridge Review* from which the pubic hair has been removed by the printer - one of my first experiences of censorship.

27

windows, with our compelling messages.

These trips would take some organising. I can remember one raid on a Labour Party conference quite vividly as it was the occasion on which we made the stew. There were twelve of us going in Fletcher's van and as nobody seemed to have any money I had the bright idea of filling a milk churn with a gigantic stew of cabbage and pigs' trotters that would sustain us through a week's agitation. There was no problem locating a milk churn, but the process of cooking the stew and decanting it by stages into the churn proved incredibly lengthy - so lengthy, in fact, that by the time the last pigs' trotters had gone in at the top those at the bottom had gone off, infecting the whole brew. We then had the problem of burying eighty pints of pigs' trotter stew in a Cambridge garden. This was done under cover of night and, to my knowledge, the stew remains buried there to this day. At some future date, no doubt, it will make a most interesting archeological find.

I never ceased to enjoy art college, but it was becoming evident that some aspects of my existence were getting up the nose of the authorities. There was much twittering among the academic staff about my living with Deirdre Amsden. In the Swinging Sixties our association would hardly have twitched an eyebrow but we were still back in the shame-ridden fifties, when appearances were deemed all important. I was made aware, from levels above Hogarth, that the fornication had to cease, lest it spread epidemic-like through the college. So we headed the problem off at the pass one lunchtime by going out and getting married. Fluck gave us a packet of twenty Senior Service as a wedding present which showed great thoughtfulness as far as I was concerned, as Deirdre did not smoke.

Then there was the matter of the Anti-Ball which Fluck and I staged in a demure village called Shelford just outside Cambridge. We got this house, one of Fletcher's about to be renovated, and did up its walls with lurid graphics naming all the destructive parties in the land - from King's College to the Monarchy. We then issued invitations for a CND fund-raiser to every activist in the country. It was without question the greatest party in Shelford's entire history but the cops still came to break it up. The whole enterprise was thought to reflect poorly on art students in general, and on the Cambridge school in particular.

I was on probation again, but I would not see the term of this one out. I was well into my final year, researching George Grosz's *Ecce Homo* series of drawings as my thesis. But certain things had changed. For one thing conscription had been abolished, so there was no chance of my being immediately presented with the Queen's Shilling on leaving college. For another, I had built up enough contacts, primarily through Fletcher and Cook, to give me some assurance of finding work. As it happened, I had to go up to London to do some research for my thesis at the British Museum. I went, and never came back.

Cartoon

Characters

For my advance on London, I wore my Cuban-heeled boots which elevated me to a shade under 6 feet 7 inches. My other accoutrements became a lime green silk shirt with flounces, and a subtle-weave grey suit with silver buttons and trumpet sleeves. I felt reasonably confident that people would see me coming.

Chapter 3

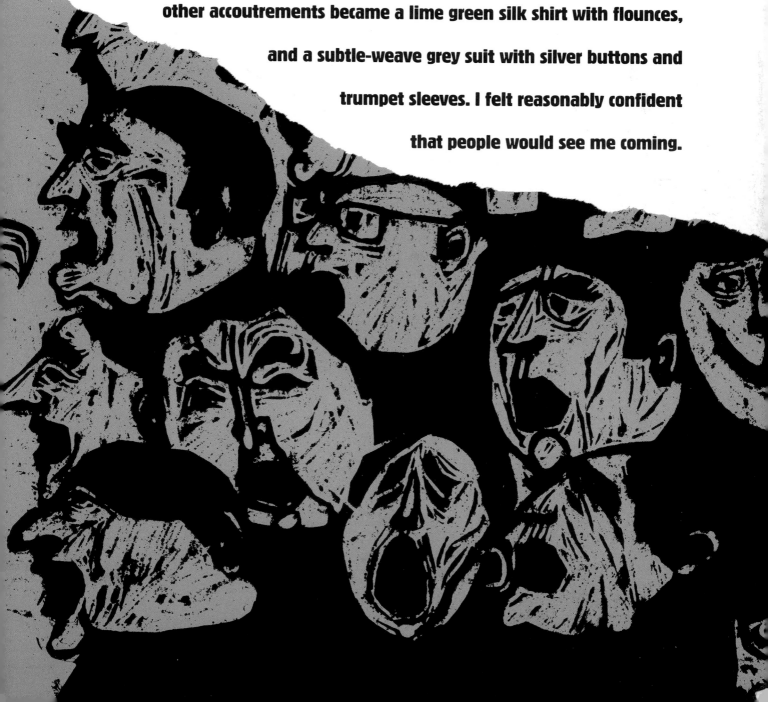

here are a number of theories about the effect of great height on personality but none, I think, are wholly satisfactory. Perhaps the most rarefied exchange on the subject was that between the liberal economist, John Kenneth Galbraith, and General Charles De Gaulle, both men in the 6' 7" league. On their first meeting De Gaulle asked Galbraith to explain his theory of height, to which the economist replied that very tall people, feeling very conspicuous from an early age, were usually better behaved than their peers and, for that reason, better fitted for leadership in later life. De Gaulle, though evidently pleased with this reply, said that Galbraith had forgotten just one thing - "Show no mercy to small men."

Perhaps because they have a few inches on me, I have been inclined to see the matter differently. It always seemed to me if you are going to be conspicuous regardless of what you do, you might as well enjoy the phenomenon by being very conspicuous. At the same time, I've never found it particularly advisable to be merciless to small men, as they are often the ones most likely to give you work.

One of the first people in London to take my work seriously was a very small man called Tom Wolsey, then the art editor of *Queen* magazine. In those days he held the unofficial title of England's Best Magazine Designer, though it turned out he had been born in Aachen. Apart from being small he was also abrupt and slightly waspish but he gave me a start with a few freelance illustration assignments.

As an introduction to the more surreal end of the communications world, *Queen* in those days could hardly be bettered. Though relatively small in circulation it was an advertising Klondike, with a readership once described as "the fresh upper crust - crumbs held together with a lot of dough". But between the glossy motoring ads it produced some very good journalism. The boss and Editor-in-Chief was Jocelyn Stevens, an outstandingly insensitive and energetic young man. He had already won an accolade from Lord Beaverbrook, the grand old man of the popular press. Beaverbrook had told a party of dinner guests, "I hear that Jocelyn Stevens bites the carpet. Now that's no bad thing."

In fact, Stevens used to bite a lot more than the carpet. The atmosphere in the *Queen* office often verged on hysteria, as Stevens raged over the Tannoy system. Debby ladies were always leaving in tears to be replaced by new debby ladies, presumably attracted by the prospect of saying over the phone, "This is the Queen speaking." On the occasion of firing his fashion editor, Stevens speeded her departure by hurling her four-drawer filing cabinet out of the window, from three floors up.

One of my assignments was to illustrate a feature article about "The New

Rich". I had assembled a wide range of sensitive studies of stockbrokers, book-makers, estate agents, auctioneers, barristers and the like, and these were ranged for inspection all over the art room floor. At this point Stevens came barging in and, with quite extraordinary precision, managed to imprint a boot mark on every single drawing. You can do wonders with fresh bread to efface marks of this kind, but not miracles. The drawings went to press with traces of the proprietor's feet still lingering.

It did not seem likely that *Queen* would be a steady enough support for me and a pregnant Deirdre even in the gypsy manner to which we had become accustomed. For the time being we were pleasantly holed up in one of Richard Fletcher's renovation projects in Drayton Gardens, Kensington. Fluck and his girlfriend (later his wife) Anne de Bruyne, another art school girl, joined us there. Then a load of other mates from college came piling in. As we could pay most of the rent by illustrating Fletcher's diatribes against the Labour right, it was all very much like old times. But it was not the kind of place, at least from a grandparent's point of view, for bringing up baby.

For a short while I even dickered with the idea of further education. Ed Middleditch, one of my tutors at college, had thought I should go on to the Royal College of Art. Middleditch was a strange, tortured man but a very powerful and intense painter, of the postwar Kitchen Sink school of artists. He was never a part of the fashionable enthusiasms at college, but he was always held in great respect. I knew that his backing for my application would count for something and, now that I had an employment record of a sort, I might even qualify for a grant.

I went to the print department of the Royal College to show my work. I could tell that academically the place had much to be said for it, because while I was waiting I fell into the company of a vague-looking young student with a most striking piece of work on a zinc plate entitled *Me and My Heroes*. It would later feature in all the reference books as David Hockney's first etching. My interview with the print-making tutor Julian Trevelyan went very well, and he asked me to start the next day. I was absolutely thrilled to be accepted by the Royal College but, even as we were confirming the time I should show up, I felt all the enthusiasm for actually going there draining out of me. I never did show up.

I think I had stumbled on the difference between an aspiration and an ambition. I genuinely did aspire to the Royal College, but my ambition, an altogether more red-blooded customer, was to get my work into newspapers. And, as it happened, the circumstances for realising this ambition suddenly became highly propitious.

By late 1961, the beginnings of boom time for satire had arrived. From its high point in 1959, with the "You've never had it so good" election, the Macmillan era was on the slide. It was apparent that Harold Macmillan, the

Left: dancing with Deirdre at the Chelsea Arts Club Ball in the Royal Albert Hall, 1958, shortly before a stink bomb explosion forced evacuation of revellers into the cold night.
Above: Aldermaston marchers: Peter Fluck, Deirdre Amsden and I assess the prospects for global peace.

Top: Fallen Angel; three studies of a journalist in the throes of creative composition. An early work for *Queen* **magazine.**

Above: part of a series of hardboard cuts with religious themes done for the wall of the Establishment Club. In this study St Francis of Assisi ministers unto the crows.

Right: "Wild Bill" Hickock, an early hardboard cut which I did for a special commemorative issue of *Granta* **magazine edited by Mark Boxer.**

"I am a moderate man ...   ... b

once accomplished old showman, was losing his touch, and the tittering in the aisles had swelled to a chorus of mockery. A revue called *Beyond the Fringe*, in which Peter Cook figured prominently, was en route for the West End where it would provide inspiration for the BBC programme *That Was the Week That Was* (later *TW3*), with David Frost as its anchor man. *Private Eye* started in business in feisty fashion and, although it would fall on hard times, Peter Cook would alleviate them by buying it up. Another Peter Cook venture was the Establishment Club in Soho, billed as London's first satirical nightclub.

Knowing Peter Cook may not have been the only qualification for advancement in the satire business but it was no drawback either. By the end of the year I was very agreeably employed as the official artist to the Establishment, responsible for filling a 14 foot by 18 inch space opposite the bar every week with a succession of monstrous ideas. Some had religious themes, like Saint Francis of Assisi being devoured by crows. But most were political. One of my favourites was of Sir Roy Welensky, then the Prime Minister of Southern Rhodesia, and a hero to that peculiar type of British person, happily more prevalent then than now, who used to rage on about the country being overrun by blacks before announcing that they were off to Africa to be among an infinitely larger number of blacks. For seven days I had Welensky, depicted as "The Whole Hog", driving the customers to drink.

The club achieved its greatest notoriety when the American comedian Lenny Bruce appeared there spraying four-letter words like confetti, which failed to conceal the fact that he was a very funny man. On one occasion a famous actress, accompanied by an early version of the toy boy, gave him a hard time, so Bruce invited her to leave, and take her son with her.

One club regular was my old friend Tom Driberg, the left-wing Labour MP, suspected at various times of working for every secret service outfit on the planet from MI5 to the KGB, and known to be the most voracious homosexual in British politics. I had first met Driberg at the Scarborough conference in

I'm prepared to fight for moderation . . .

if necessary I'll go the whole hog."

SIR ROY WELENSKY

1960, at one of those hotel functions that let the agitators in. We got on famously, though I was not entirely unaware of the reasons for Driberg's interest in me. Nor, it appeared, was Barbara Castle, who happened to notice that there was a handbag left on a chair behind where we were standing. She picked it up, turned to me with a sweet smile, and said: "Is this yours, dear?"

As it turned out, Driberg became a very good friend to both Fluck and myself without being granted any sexual favours. It was Driberg who lifted Fluck up from the drudgery of paste-up work at *Private Eye* to the eminence of "artist reporter" work for the *New Statesman*, and he provided me with a never-ending stream of funny ideas for my space on the wall. We used to say that the great thing about Driberg was that he was so corrupt that he was incorruptible.

There were certain penalties in the friendship. It was impossible, for example, to go anywhere with him without it being assumed that you were his boyfriend. But I always thought it was a very modest price to pay for the pleasure of his company. However I would start to pay a larger price, particularly when Driberg came to look to me for companionship on his jaunts to places that made him slightly nervous.

I was particularly in demand when he went down to the East End at the invitation of his gangster mates, Ronald and Reginald Kray. I can remember the first time very well as the twins thoughtfully came round to the House of Commons in a Rolls-Royce to pick up Driberg and myself. We were installed in the back seat with our hosts and the man next to the driver turned to me and said, in deepest cockney guttural, "Would you like a scar?" Luckily, Driberg was able to translate the threat as a friendly offer of a cigar.

These events in the East End were jolly but more than slightly unnerving. There would be a lot of sports and showbiz people being encouraged to have a good time by the Krays. So a good time was a very smart thing to have. Around the twins themselves, there was an extraordinary air of impending vio-

"The Whole Hog": a cartoon series based on Sir Roy Welensky who, as Prime Minister of Southern Rhodesia, flew the flag for white supremacy in Africa. First shown on the wall of the Establishment Club at a width of 14 feet, later produced, on a more modest scale, in *Queen* magazine.

lence and, of course, as the lurid details of their trial would eventually reveal, there were a number of individuals against whom the violence did not merely impend. But with Driberg they were solicitude itself. There would always be a young man, usually of a slightly effeminate nature, assigned to keep him entertained. The tragedy of it was that Driberg never managed to summon up the courage to tell the Krays that he did not much care for effeminate men. He liked lorry drivers and policemen, the hunkier the better.

In the summer of 1962 the *Observer* gave its grave accolade to satire by establishing a new page imaginatively called "Satire" to differentiate it from the rest of the product. Peter Cook and Michael Frayn were the main writers, while Cook and I produced a running cartoon strip under the prophetic title "Almost the End". The progress of the new page was keenly watched by the *Observer*'s patrician Editor, David Astor, though most of my practical dealings were with George Seddon, one of the livelier executives. On the strength of Seddon's commission, Deirdre and I moved to a flat of our own in Peter Street, Soho, with our newborn baby son, Shem. To judge by the nature of the surrounding establishments we would not have to waste an enormous amount of time teaching him the facts of life.

My orderly progress into journalism very nearly came unstuck with the events of the Cuban missile crisis. For a few weeks in October, as the Russians and the Americans played their lunatic game of nuclear "chicken", there was what amounted to mob rule in parts of the West End of London. What were conceived as orderly demonstrations soon degenerated into free-for-alls. There were reports of extreme hotheads going around torching police motorcycles, which I knew to be true as I set one alight myself.

More perilously, I got involved outside the American Embassy when two youngsters darted into the street to stop a police wagon. A police sergeant got out and really laid into these two kids, so I laid into the police sergeant and knocked him down. Then a load of other policemen came piling out of the wagon, tripping over one another like Keystone Cops. I must have hit another four of them before I legged it down the road.

They caught me and took me to Cannon Row police station, by which time I was blubbing on a grand scale. Assault and battery of five police officers was not going to be just another £5 fine with an admonishment to be good in future. But the police were in a funny mood, not just about the incident, which arguably they had started, but about the whole situation. I realised with some surprise, though it should have been obvious, that the cops were as scared about the nuclear showdown as anyone else and that, on one level at least, they were glad that people were demonstrating against it. I blubbed on for a couple of hours before they decided to drop the assault charges and do me for rioting which then carried a nominal fine. At the court hearing, I saw one of the policemen, all strapped up. "You bastard," he said. "If I'd known what you'd done to

THE
OBSERVER

ALMOST THE END

NEW SATIRICAL PAGE WITH

· **Michael Frayn**
· **Peter Cook**
· **Roger Law**

PRINTED BY F.A.H. LTD. WORSHIP STREET, E.C.2

Advertising bill poster for the *Observer's* first satire page.

me, I wouldn't have dropped the charges. You've cracked two of my ribs."

But their leniency, if regretted, was not entirely misplaced. For the first time in my relations with the police, I felt I seriously owed them one. I never waded into them with the same relish ever again.

This was not quite the end of my fighting days. In fact, I was involved in a major brawl only a few weeks later with one of the rather unsatirical heavies that were infiltrating the Establishment Club in increasing numbers. Ostensibly I got the better of it but when I got home Deirdre said, "What's happened to your coat?" I took the coat off and it was like a Chinese lantern, with long slashes all down the front. I had never even realised my opponent had a razor. I had just learned another important lesson, which was that London brawlers had much less respect for the Queensberry Rules than their country cousins in Cambridgeshire.

Chapter 4

My first cartoon strip in a national newspaper, concocted in collaboration with Peter Cook, was directed at a brace of soft targets, Hugh Gaitskell and George Brown. We had a frazzled-looking Labour leader imploring his hard-eyed henchman to stop calling him "Brother" because, "It reminds me so much of the Labour Party."

After such a modest start, the Observer was convinced that we were bound to improve. And we did, quite rapidly. It was not very long before Cook produced his deathless critical observation: "I go to the theatre to be entertained. I don't want to see plays about rape, sodomy and drug addiction - I can get all that at home."

Putting Armageddon on Hold

Roger Law | Peter Cook

ALMOST THE EN

y own high point came in the wake of a news story about a man being birched in prison. I illustrated this theme by having the then Home Secretary, Rab Butler, discussing flogging with his wife in an English country garden while lopping the heads off tulips with his cane. This brought my work to the direct attention of the Editor. David Astor told me that he rather liked the tulip-chopping image, but he was outraged by my inclusion of the Home Secretary's wife in the joke. He told me that in attacking public figures I had to learn how to distinguish between the public and the private in their lives, but I don't think I ever did.

It was curtains for the "Almost the End" strip but Astor, being an exceptionally humane man, allowed me to stay on. I was put on a two day a week retainer and allocated a tiny attic office on the Tudor Street premises. From this pleasant niche, I launched a vigorous assault on the freelance market though, out of consideration for my kindly employer, I would only do an occasional drawing for its main rival, the *Sunday Times*, under an assumed name.

There was still plenty of work to be done for *Queen*, though my original patron Tom Wolsey had been let go by Jocelyn Stevens with characteristic panache. Stevens had rushed into Wolsey's vacated office and set about it with bucket and mop while muttering incantations about washing that man right out of his hair. Wolsey, of course, was far too talented to remain on the cobbles for very long and he bounced back almost immediately as the art editor of *Town*, another attractive glossy of the day. So I worked for *Queen* and *Town* and when *Town* acquired a stablemate called *Topic*, a doomed attempt to produce a British *Newsweek*, I worked for that too.

"You know, I go to the theatre to be entertained . . .

I don't want to see plays about rape, sodomy and drug addiction . . .

I can get all that at home."

For a while *Town* was edited by Nick Tomalin, a superb young writer who would eventually be killed while covering the Yom Kippur war for the *Sunday Times*. But what impressed me about Tomalin at the time was not his writing skill so much as his ability to inflame Wolsey. I remember walking in on a blazing row between them over some design problem in which Wolsey expressed his dissent by removing Tomalin's hat and coat from the coatstand, placing them carefully on the floor, and then jumping up and down on them.

Until 1964 there were no colour supplements in the newspapers aside from the *Sunday Times* and even that was struggling to master the technique of printing back-to-back colour. So the established colour magazines like *Queen* and *Town* were really quite influential. Of the two I tended to prefer *Town*, which was part of the Haymarket Press combine owned by two rising young thrusters called Michael Heseltine and Clive Labovitch (more popularly known as "Vaseline" and "Lavatory Brush"). The main part of the empire was devoted to business magazines, produced by hordes of young journalists in conditions that would give a battery hen claustrophobia. In contrast, *Town* was an indulged area, though a shrinking one.

It had originally been called *Man about Town*, which subsequently became *About Town*, so after the foreshortening to *Town* it really had no place to go. But before it died it made some forays into serious journalism and I was able to brush up my "artist reporting" skills on subjects slightly less frivolous than those that tended to come my way from *Queen*. My most serious assignment, however, came from the current affairs magazine, *Topic*, which asked me to do a cover showing what life, or the lack of it, would be like after a nuclear holocaust.

None of this freelance activity required neglect of my duties at the *Observer*, as these were not onerous. Having established to David Astor's satisfaction that I was not to be trusted in the official mockery squad, I tended to be

Left: the high point of the low humour that characterised the "Almost the End" cartoon strip. Words by Peter Cook.

Below: the cartoon strip that offended David Astor, the Editor of the *Observer*, and led to my redeployment on other duties. Words by Peter Cook.

Peter Cook and Roger Law react to this news item—

FRANK MITCHELL, a 33-year-old prisoner serving a life sentence for robbery with violence, was given 15 strokes of the birch in Hull prison yesterday for attacking two officers.

A Home Office statement said that eight prisoners, including Mitchell, escaped from prison on April 23.

escort, grabbed an officer by the throat and slashed him with a sharpened tin knife. The officer received cuts to both sides of the face requiring 22 stitches.

Mitchell has escaped from Broadmoor and Rampton. He was declared sane at Reading Assizes in 1958 and sentenced to life imprisonment for robbing a 64-year-old man with violence during a two-day escape from Broadmoor.

Now you know how I dislike violence, Mollie . . .

but this man is impossible. They did everything they could for him at Rampton and Broadmoor, but he kept escaping and assaulting people. I really believe that this birching will be a deterrent . . .

If he does it again he must be off his head.

Right: original artwork for the *Observer* cartoon strip. Peter Cook, in the interests of topicality, believed in delivering the words late, so the artwork often had to be done overnight. This accounts for its unpolished, jigsaw-like appearance.

Below: the current affairs magazine, *Topic*, featured my woodcut of Herr Ulbricht, the East German premier, on its cover as a late replacement for my study of Armageddon which was put on hold until the end of the world seemed more imminent.

but when I think of his appalling long hair....

and his ridiculous Teddy Boy costume

ver they say you can still tell a lot by outward

rances.

deployed on pure illustration work, doing the drawings for other people's articles. As most of the other people were interesting, this was usually agreeable work. The place was full of wise older brothers and uncles who could tell you any number of things you didn't know, and it was not entirely deficient in a pleasant class of young tearaway. One of the nicest of them, a youngster from Finsbury Park called Don McCullin, was already on the road to becoming the world's greatest war photographer since Robert Capa.

My own outdoor assignments were, happily, less dangerous but not without their perils. Many of these occurred in association with Jeremy Sandford, an upper-class writer absorbed by what he saw as working-class culture. Sandford would write an excellent television play about homelessness called *Cathy Come Home* but during my period with him he was more concerned with the workers at play. Thus I would find myself marooned in fun-loving places like Majorca and Clacton-on-Sea, eternally waiting for Sandford to show up.

My worst experience was in a Butlins camp where, quartered with the young folk, there was a terrible outbreak of chalet rash - the camp name for love bites. The noise level of after-dark activity got so intense that, after four sleepless nights, I begged to be relocated with the old age pensioners. Next morning Sandford bounced in full of beans and bouquets for the culture - "I do love the plastic parrots here, don't you Roger? You must have been having the most wonderful time." I refrained from throttling him. Sandford's journeys through the working-class at play would subsequently be reproduced in book form, with my drawings as illustration. I don't think it represented a pinnacle of achievement for either of us, but the title wasn't bad. It was called *Synthetic Fun*.

My work on the *Observer* helped me to evolve techniques that best suited my skill. Pencil drawings in newspaper illustrations were almost invariably reproduced in half-tone blocks, and very nondescript they could look too. To get round this, I would draw on very thin lay-out paper spread over a thick cartridge paper with a strong grain in it, and this would give the effect of a broken line, perfect for reproduction as the much stronger and sharper line blocks. I was a long way from being the best draughtsman in the newspaper business but I liked to think that nobody else could make their stuff leap so far off the page.

The most significant political event during my time at the *Observer* was the election in 1964 of a new Labour government led by Harold Wilson. This was a body-blow for satire, which had gorged itself on the Profumo Affair and Tory decline. But there was, even on the far Left, a feeling that with a new dawn of political wisdom, satire would no longer be necessary. I did not share the optimism on this point, because there was something that troubled me about Harold Wilson. I couldn't help it, I just did not like his face. In those days I thought it possible that I was being unfair, but I later discovered a powerful precedent for this form of political analysis. While the American Civil War was

Below: Waistcoat with mother of pearl stitched on in small squares. A unique find in the Portobello Road. Hand-tailored shirt. Black trousers, slightly flared

Below: Turn of the century black tailcoat. Plain Edwardian waistcoat. Victorian watch chain complete with fourpenny pieces. Subhuman jacket with

Below: Astrakhan waisted frock coat. High winged collar and large black tie. Striped trousers, well cut in formal city style

Right: Old-school straw boater. Hand-tailored lightweight suit based on an Edwardian gent's summerwear; cream with charcoal grey stitching, worn without effort to accentuate the suit's period characteristics. A high-collared white shirt, a fancy bow tie, preferably spotted—silver-topped canes are lucky finds in markets and junk shops

No one quite knows how it started though the general feeling is that a few bright lads, home from 6th form and university for the holidays, got bored with dirty jeans. Without the funds for Carnaby Street they looked for, and are still finding, grandpa's frock coat and Dad's wedding outfit. Those without attics search the markets (Portobello Road; Brixton; Church St., Paddington); those with the dosh (the fun has spread to young men who work in, on and around magazines, art departments, television and films)

are having things made by the sort of tailors who are amazed at nothing. The basically conservative keep their finery—which is regarded as something between dandyism and fancy-dress—for Friday and Saturday night parties. The extroverts, in sympathetic employment, wear it to work. What's wanted: Victorian and Edwardian tail coats, particularly the city gent's coat of charcoal frieze with braid buttons. These have the advantage in that, having been made for portly men, they fit the boys across the shoulders. Edwardian

day suits are usually too narrow and have to be made. Stiff collars are got from barrows (1s. in a fair price). Waistcoats—fancy, pearl grey, dark with braid buttons—change hands at about 5s. and the fact that most are too short and end around the ribs doesn't seem to matter. Mothers with lace-boxes part with lengths of Honiton for Highland-style jabots, and tie pins, watch chains, silver-headed canes are sought by perfectionists

Drawings by Roger Law

raging, Abraham Lincoln rejected an excellently qualified Ministerial candidate on the grounds that he did not like his face. When reproved by his aides for vetoing an appointment on such flimsy grounds, Lincoln observed: "Every man over forty is responsible for his own face."

As the *Observer* was easily the most liberal of the quality Sunday newspapers, it might be thought that it would be the one most energised by the election of a Labour government. This did not prove to be the case. Things puttered on in the old paternalistic way. It was said that there was no human foible that the editor could not understand, so if I managed to stay out of jail I was confronted with the possibility of a job for life.

The sense of security would probably have been less oppressive had it not been for the fact that the *Sunday Times*, once considered a tired old Tory rag, was acquiring a wildly exciting reputation. Its by now stylish colour magazine easily eclipsed the clumsy new productions of the *Observer* and the *Telegraph*, while its news section was becoming famous for something called "the beer bottle school of journalism", which would write, edit and design right through Friday night in order to trounce the opposition. Within the scholastic portals of the *Observer* all this frantic activity in the enemy camp was rather frowned upon. But the young hopefuls on the payroll all started to twitch.

Peter Dunn, the *Observer*'s best young reporter, was the first to defect, and he would be followed, after a short interval, by Don McCullin and myself.

My first and last fashion drawings for *Vogue* magazine, sensitively designed and laid-out by David King.

47

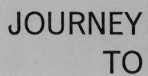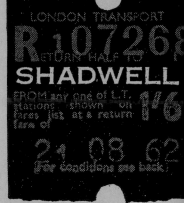

JOURNEY TO SHADWELL

ARTIST'S report from London's East End dockland by ROGER LAW

Artist reporting at home and abroad. Right: a series of drawings for the *Observer* of Shadwell, then - and now, as it happens - a depressed district in the East End of London with more life in it than it deserved. Above: a Majorca study, one of many drawings I did to illustrate articles by Jeremy Sandford on his long probe into the British working classes at play.

KOSHER BUTCHERS, HESSEL STREET

ITALIAN STALL OWNER

NEGRO WORKER

FLATS IN SHADWELL, E.1

CAFÉ AT WAPPING WALL

WATCHER ON THE STAIRS

CHILDREN AT PLAY IN WATNEY ST.

Annu
now

DOWN
TO
EARTH

BY sowing the
at bulb-plan
grow earlier, str
plants than thos
spring.

Cornflowers are
insurance against
and they can be so
October, whereas
annuals need Se
Cornflowers can r
wallflowers and for
bulb border. The
May to Septembe
dying foliage of da
and Spanish iris le
grass. (Cut the d
bulb iris so that they
in seeding but incre
naturalised in g
dwindling each year

The bushiest cor
foot-high *Centaur*
Polka Dot mixtur
blues, lavenders and
kinds—dark blue J
Gem and Lilac La
compact. Double
Carmine Rose an
grow 3 to 4 ft. h
sowing and exce
corners need cane
strings between.

More love, le

Dig in compost
mould with 4 oz
square yard to fee
annuals. Sow in fu
and 15 inches apar
a foot apart for P

September sowir
which should be th
over 4 feet high f
back of the borde
vases in July and
Regal or Supreme
mum height, Gian
named varieties fo

Love-in-a-mist s
grows a sturdy
canes, flowering fro
ber, spaced a foo
The new *Nigella*
"mist" and more
Jekyll, with vivid
inches across, red s
shapely seed vessel
flower arrangemen

Though clarkia a
sown in autumn, t
in June, but ann
its 3 to 4 feet
pincushion flowers
reds and pinks,
finishes with the fr
inch deep, thinning

Indian Pinks sov
September make
carpet at this sp
scarlet Bravo, Fir
the many mixtu
sinensis blaze from
and make it perhap
ing small annual

**Next
Advice o
PATRICK**

Chapter 5 I was recruited to the Sunday Times by Michael Rand, the art editor of its new colour magazine, whom I already knew as a man of considerable resource. For one thing he had reached his level of visual eminence with only one functioning eye; for another he had been responsible for the famous "Expressograph" feature when he worked with the Daily Express. This was a skilful compilation of graphs and diagrams which helped to persuade readers of a number of comforting patriotic propositions, like how the British nuclear deterrent was superior to the American one, and so on. Rand made it clear to me that I, too, should be flexible. I was to work for both the newspaper and the magazine, and I had to be ready

to draw anything from a sampan to a sausage in five minutes flat.

From a Sampan to a Sausage

Photograph: Robert Freeson

BUTTERED
POPPED
CORN

he *Sunday Times* had a very strong team of news photographers but there were certain areas that they either could not reach or felt disinclined to penetrate. So I would get to do the news drawings for things like Chinese gambling dens, where the photographers were likely to get their cameras smashed, and big courtroom scenes, where cameramen were not allowed to take pictures. As it happens, drawing was not allowed either, but you could make a fair stab of it by going along and making a few doodles in your pocket and then doing the composition from memory later.

On one of these jobs I was allowed to penetrate backstairs at the Old Bailey, where I was fascinated to discover a system of light switches as intricate as anything you might find in the rear end of a Drury Lane theatre. Behind the majesty of the law there was a scrupulous attention to special effects. I was naturally a critic of all the flummery and pedantry of courtroom proceedings, though much less so after I had been sent to draw Myra Hindley and Ian Brady at the Moors Murders trial. On that occasion I was actually grateful for the artificiality of it all, as a means of taking the edge off the horror under discussion.

I got to know the top brass on the *Sunday Times* quite quickly, less through my own efforts than because I shared an office with David Hillman, a fantastically meticulous young designer who used to do the Review Front, the main features showcase of the newspaper that was always vetted at the top level. Hardly a week would go by without Hillman hammering the desk with his metal rule and threatening to resign over how the insensitive journalists were butchering his magnificent constructions. And I would have to pad along the corridors of power seeking compromise solutions.

Most of my real work was done for the magazine, where my immediate boss was David King, the associate art editor and the real designing genius of the enterprise. King was just twenty-two, a year younger than myself, and unusual in a number of respects. He had an unnerving cackling laugh and spoke with a wheezy cockney intonation that suggested three lifetimes spent on sixty gaspers a day. Strangers would invariably find him disconcerting. Once, when hospitalised after a serious car accident, a doctor told King's wife, Philomena, that she should brace herself for a shock when seeing him as it was unlikely that he would ever be the same man again. After seeing her husband, Mrs King was able to reassure the doctor - he had always been like that.

On any magazine the relationship between the illustrator and the designer is crucial to its appearance and mine with King was already very good. On emerging from the London College of Printing as the hot-shot typographer of his generation, King had done postgraduate studies in obstreperous behaviour by working closely with Tom Wolsey at both *Queen* and *Town*. He had even

flashed through at the *Observer* but left after a few weeks, raging at "Duffle-coat designers" who didn't know a headline from a hole in the wall. King's judgements were of a quite astonishing rapidity and for the most part astonishingly acute, though they were assisted by his ability to discard vast acreages of artistic experience as being "boring". He believed that Mark Rothko was the greatest artist since Rembrandt, and possibly since before that. I remember one distinguished illustrator, who had shown King his work, making a loud moan about its being dismissed "in five minutes".

"Five minutes," said King, when reproached later for being so abrupt. "It didn't take ten seconds."

Our most intimate association, prior to the *Sunday Times*, had been on *Magnet News*, billed as Britain's first black newspaper, for which King had devised the biggest logo in creation. The launch was announced from the Commonwealth Institute where we met Malcom X, the American black militant leader, and I could not help noticing that for a man fond of describing white people as "blue-eyed devils" he had an interesting facial feature - very blue eyes. King and I had a lot of fun putting the newspaper together but after the first issue they let the white men go. Shortly afterwards, they let everybody go. But it was the bold design of *Magnet News* that first led Michael Rand to suspect that we might have something to offer the *Sunday Times*.

King's mandate on the magazine was to make it look livelier - a golden opportunity for a man who wanted to smuggle pop newspaper, and later pop art, techniques into the quality press - and a lot more colourful, which was

Michael Rand, art editor of the *Sunday Times* magazine, making a pot, flanked by other admiring magazine heavies. Left to right: David Sylvester, art critic; David King, designer, and George Perry, film buff and writer.
Photograph: Ian Yeomans

**The Sunday Times
art department
posing as a pop group**

David King

The designer, telling the
group how it's going to be

David Barnes

The assistant designer,
giving a careful ear

Roger Law

The illustrator, wondering where the next pint is coming from.

David Hillman

The visiting newspaper designer, politely laughing it off.

Gilvrie Misstear

King's right hand, helpless with mirth.

Photograph: Ian Yeomans

Flexibility in hardboard cuts.
Above: illustration for the diaries
of Harold Nicolson in the *Sunday
Times* Review Front.
Right: depiction of the LSD
injection episode in Len
Deighton's novel, *An Expensive
Place to Die*, for a serialisation in
Nova magazine.
Far right: representation of
Salvatore Giuliano, the Sicilian
Bandit King, for the *Sunday
Times* magazine feature "The
Lost Heroes".

Law Courts

My most majestic day in court was made possible by a *Sunday Times* inquiry into the law. This picture, above, of me adjudicating at the Old Bailey was taken by Deirdre Amsden, and was an unofficial spin-off from an illustration assignment which we carried out with Richard Weigand.

Strangely, this picture never appeared in the *Sunday Times*, though the model of the courtroom, above right, made by Richard Weigand, was given some prominence.

Drawing and model-making were not exactly encouraged when a court was in session. But, unlike photography, it was hard to proscribe absolutely. I used to go along to big cases and do some doodles in my pocket which would provide the basis for larger constructions, and sometimes models, when I got back to the office.

I was a critic of all the flummery of court proceedings but this did not interfere with my pleasure in doing the work. Indeed, I would seek it out as much as possible and find drama in even the most elementary cases.

During my early years in the newspaper business I drew a lot of courtrooms, criminals and judges like the two characters, right, who featured in the *Observer*. One of the simple joys of drawing court scenes was that you could get on with the work in the office without someone com-

ing along and saying there was a photograph which would illustrate the subject much better. It was a small, but secure, niche for the artist reporter. I also enjoyed the work for the opportunity it gave me to go to court without being among those in the dock, though any enjoyment was hard to sustain after the *Sunday Times* sent me to cover the Moors Murders trial as its artist reporter.

Photographs: above left, Deirdre Amsden; above right, Ian Yeomans.

Top right: *Magnet News,*
published in February 1965, was
billed as Britain's first black
newspaper. Due to a shortage of
black designers and illustrators in
those days (happily now being
repaired), responsibility for the
paper's appearance was entrusted to David King and myself. Jan
Carew, the playwright and
publisher of the paper, relieved
us of the responsibility after the
first issue in order to bring on
more authentically black talent.
The newspaper had a short but
spirited life. Below: my son
Shem, aged three, in a bedroom
evidently shaped by the influence
of *Magnet News.*

partly where I came in. One of the major problems with the early magazine was that while it had access to so many exciting new colour processes through its press in Watford, most of the best stories would still resolutely come in as black and white. This was partly because most of the best stock pictures were monochrome and partly because some of the very best photographers, Don McCullin being a prime example, were averse to shooting in colour. As a counterbalance to this, King thought the magazine should inject much more colour into its illustrations. Since I had developed a line in garish woodcuts - more specifically hardboard cuts - along with my drawing, I was well fitted to assist in this enterprise. The brash background colour for these works could be effortlessly inserted in the form of instructions to the printer.

King made a point of getting to know the potential of the technology at Watford and, as a result, soon began to come up with ideas for beefing up the appearance of photo-stories that still had to be in black and white. He started introducing four-colour black into the magazine and this would give the pictures much greater depth on the page. It was an expensive improvement but, as King was fond of pointing out, spending to keep the *Observer* and *Telegraph* magazines thrashing about in our wake was doing the proprietor an enormous favour.

Without realising my luck, I had moved from boom time for satire to boom time for the newspaper business. Looking back, it's apparent that the mid-sixties period of the *Sunday Times* was the most creative phase in newspapers since the war. This was the time when the Insight column was born, and at its best, and when every traditional rule about how a quality paper should look was broken and remade. Other newspapers would pay it the compliment of aping its methods. It seemed as if a general advance in the freedom and authority of the press was being made. It was only later that we realised it was a freak occurrence.

Perhaps the most freakish aspect of the newspaper in those days was having a proprietor who did not interfere. Though no moral giant, Lord Thomson knew how to delegate. The other peculiarity was the age range. Aside from a thin layer of avuncular figures who had been in submarines and Spitfires in the war and were located at the very top, it was hard to find anybody there over thirty-five. Indeed, most of the high-pressure jobs in the newsroom and departments like Insight were done by people in their twenties.

This was partly a product of expansion, but it also had to be a consequence of a deliberate hiring policy. On the *Sunday Times* this alliance between the war generation and the new generation was a key source of energy, and I suspect that it was the main factor behind many areas of sixties creativity. While a lot of youth there were having their way, there were also a lot of shrewd old buzzards allowing them to have it. On the *Sunday Times* the shrewdest of them all was Denis Hamilton, an editor of almost painful reticence who had served on Montgomery's staff during the war. Hamilton was succeeded by Harry Evans, a more charismatic figure, and newspaper histories tend to give Evans most credit for the emergence of the *Sunday Times* as a great newspaper. But he only drove the engine, albeit brilliantly. It was Hamilton who built it.

Although the newspaper had a lot of bustle, there were certain still centres. One of them was Godfrey Smith, the Editor of the magazine, who probably delegated even more efficiently than Lord Thomson. Most of the magazine's ideas emerged from a "think tank" he set up and which usually consisted of Rand, King, the writer Francis Wyndham and the fashion editor Meriel McCooey. In consequence, Smith was able to sit behind a desk without a single scrap of paper on it. If, however, you had to go and see his deputy, you had to take a machete to the files in his office to get at him.

Even so, Smith was more than a diplomat. Whenever a difficult decision

came up, like whether Don McCullin's brilliant but harrowing pictures from Vietnam should be allowed to spoil the reader's breakfast, he almost invariably came down on the side of the radicals.

One of my first major jobs for Smith was a series of drawings for Graham Greene's novel *The Comedians*, which was serialised in the magazine. They were done in sombre shades of green, brown and grey and were not unsubtle, to my mind. They were even reviewed in the *Journal* of the Hornsey School of Art, where I had done some teaching in my loafing days at the *Observer*. "I feel," said the reviewer, "that Roger Law has extended himself beyond his resources, rather like someone trying to play Wagner on a Jew's harp."

I had more popular success when Chris Stamp of Track Records commissioned David King and myself to do a couple of record covers - one for Jimi Hendrix, and another for The Who. The image we created for the Hendrix cover subsequently became the best-selling poster of the decade, but The Who assignment posed the more interesting problems, as it involved persuading Roger Daltry to immerse himself up to his armpits in a bath of cold baked beans to achieve the desired artistic effect.

I enjoyed these diversions from mainstream journalism without seeing them as a serious alternative to the real thing. But at the same time, my conception of the real thing was changing. Without being any way dissatisfied with the paper, I knew there would be no repetition of the great days of "artist reporting" as defined by Paul Hogarth. In the modern world it could only really start where photography left off, and photography could now go practically everywhere. Illustration might still be important to a newspaper's overall appearance, but it was not something you found people discussing in pubs, unless they happened to be other illustrators.

There was still a place for great draughtsmanship of course, like that produced by two near contemporaries of mine, Gerald Scarfe and Ralph Steadman. But I was never going to be able to draw as well as those two characters. I realised that if I was ever going to excite the regulars in the Pig and Whistle, I would have to come up with something else.

Peter Fluck and I had discussed the possibility of model-making for profit at college but, as there did not seem to be any demand, nothing got made. Then, in the summer of 1966, a small window of journalistic opportunity swung open. *Nova*, which was one of the livelier magazines around, asked me to illustrate a feature about Catholicism with something a bit different. So I modelled a priest and a penitent in plasticine, and we established communication between them by cutting a hole in the page. The heads were crudely modelled and only adequately photographed, but they were novel enough to win a Design and Art Directors' Association award.

I did not capitalise on this modest breakthrough with any great speed, because an American adventure intervened.

Cover for *The Who Sell Out* album, 1967, produced by David King and myself. We had no problem getting Pete Townshend to shove a king-size deodorant up his armpit, but persuading Roger Daltry to immerse himself in a bath of cold baked beans required diplomatic skills of the highest order.

Photograph: David Montgomery

THE WHO SELL OUT

Replacing the stale smell of excess with
the sweet smell of success,
Peter Townshend, who, like nine out of ten star
needs it. Face the music with Odorono,
the all-day deodorant
that turns perspiration into inspiration.

THE WHO SELL OUT

This way to a cowboy's breakfast.
Daltry rides again. Thinks: "Thanks to Heinz
Baked Beans everyday is a super day".
Those who know how many beans make five
get Heinz beans inside and outside at
every opportunity. Get saucy.

The priest, left, and the penitent, above right, in communication through a hole in the page, were commissioned in 1966 by Dennis Hackett, the Editor of *Nova*, to illustrate an article about Catholicism. My first plasticine models are clearly works of a rough-hewn quality, but they were sufficiently surprising at the time to win a Design and Art Directors' Association award. In the same period I modelled a likeness of Frank Sinatra, below, for a special show at Madame Tussaud's. His head would be mounted on a ball-jointed body and exhibited in a 14-foot champagne glass I made out of two helicopter bubbles.

Photograph: Sally Soames

Chapter 6 I may well owe my American experience to the Central Intelligence Agency. Some years ago it was revealed that the CIA had secretly channelled funds to the various foundations who made a speciality of subsidising European students and scholars visiting the United States. The thinking behind this was that your average anti-American, educated, young lefty from Europe would, on exposure to the country, be so feeble-minded as to fall in love with the place and become pro-American for evermore. It was a cynical, manipulative policy, but in my case it was almost wholly effective.

A Joint Too Far

Bearer
Titulaire

my invitation to take up a teaching post as artist-in-residence at Reed College in Portland, Oregon, came from James Webb, a member of the faculty there who, in an earlier incarnation, had been one of my editors on *Granta* in Cambridge. The Rockefeller Foundation then came through with a grant sufficient to support me and my family for six months. We were now, with the birth of Sophie, four in number, but still highly mobile. We had never exactly put down deep roots in London having lived at five different addresses, ranging from Soho to Notting Hill Gate, in five years. So another move, even to the far side of the United States, was no major wrench.

I took up my academic duties in the autumn of 1967, while Lyndon Baines Johnson was still President and the country was in turmoil over the war in Vietnam. In the London we had just left, dissent against the war was still very much a preserve of the radical left. Wilson's Labour government was firmly pro-Johnson on the grounds of having to show loyalty to the Americans. In Oregon, there was scarcely a loyal American in sight on the subject of the war, while on campus at Reed, positive hostility tended to prevail.

This partly stemmed from its radical tradition. The institution was founded by the John Reed who wrote *Ten Days that Shook the World*, a celebration of the Bolshevik revolution in Russia. But the more important reason for dismay at the war, not only at Reed but on all the American campuses, was the havoc it was playing with the academic system. Everyone knew that a young man's

ejection from college amounted to conscription for a war growing more unpopular by the minute and in this situation the marking of male students became utterly bizarre. There were a few tutors who did not succumb to the temptation to give high marks to the lowest achievers, but I was not one of them.

The other serious temptation I succumbed to was drugs. Though I deliberately refrained from LSD and sticking needles up my arm, I took full advantage of the wide range of speed and marijuana on offer. I cannot say that ingestion of these substances actually improved my work, but the amphetamines certainly enabled me to tap sources of energy I had not previously been aware of. However, after one episode when my heart seemed to be making a great effort to leap out of my body, I came to use speed very sparingly. My experiences with marijuana were much more benign and led to some interesting encounters.

One of these was with Howard Rheingold who used to attend campus events dressed as a cockroach. In human form Rheingold had tight blond curls and blackcurrant black eyes which were always fixed on some lunatic proposition. One of his experiments, in which I was very happy to participate, involved getting very seriously stoned. Then, when you were in this condition, Rheingold would couple you up to his machine - an arrangement of wires which would dangle from your head and led to a screen which flashed up your Alpha rhythms.

As the experiment developed you would have to try to reproduce these same Alpha rhythms without the benefit of drugs, and you would do this by learning certain in-brain entertainment techniques. To some extent it could actually be done, but the cumbersome technology prevented wider application. It was always Rheingold's ambition to get the whole thing down to the size of a wristwatch, so that Wall Street businessmen could stone themselves while commuting to work. We naturally all thought that Rheingold was as mad as a cockroach but I notice that he is now the Editor of the *Whole Earth Review,* a highly respected environmental publication, and the author of a best-selling work about advanced computer applications, called *Virtual Reality*. He also regularly gives evidence on techno-ecological matters to Congressional Committees, and is listened to with the utmost respect.

My only official duty at Reed was teaching students illustration, but I had a drug-induced notion that it might be fun to make a puppet film with the help of student volunteers and Will Baker, an English lecturer from Boise, Idaho, who taught in a cowboy hat. The basic idea was to construct a little team of marionettes who would act out the life of a family of the future. This family's chief characteristic would be that it had completely come to terms with consumer society. Everything about them had to be standardised down to the number of children, which in America at that time was 2.4. We were

Above: a letter to my son Shem from the land of opportunity.
Left: James Webb, professor of English Literature and a popular guru figure at Reed College, Oregon, who invited me to become the college's artist-in-residence.
Far left: a West Coast education; four Reed College students plus one unidentified party pictured at a swimming stop in Marin County, California. The student in the foreground is Howard Rheingold, the three figures in the background, from left to right, are Linda Burnham, Gary Achziger and John Reynall.
Photograph: Roger Law

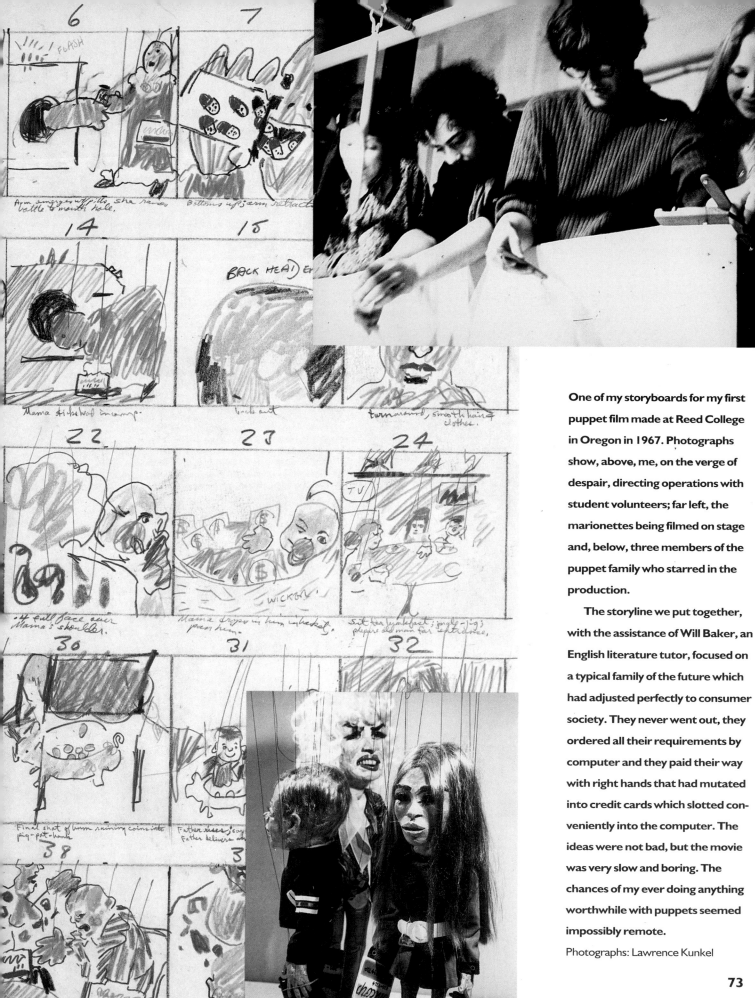

One of my storyboards for my first puppet film made at Reed College in Oregon in 1967. Photographs show, above, me, on the verge of despair, directing operations with student volunteers; far left, the marionettes being filmed on stage and, below, three members of the puppet family who starred in the production.

The storyline we put together, with the assistance of Will Baker, an English literature tutor, focused on a typical family of the future which had adjusted perfectly to consumer society. They never went out, they ordered all their requirements by computer and they paid their way with right hands that had mutated into credit cards which slotted conveniently into the computer. The ideas were not bad, but the movie was very slow and boring. The chances of my ever doing anything worthwhile with puppets seemed impossibly remote.

Photographs: Lawrence Kunkel

73

Top: Deirdre Amsden operates the Mama character I modelled for the puppet film.
Below: the puppet film set.
Right: my life-sized model of the singer Janis Joplin. Her ardent fan is just discernible on the right of the picture.
Photographs: Above, Lawrence Kunkel; Right, David Montgomery

unable to think of a way of conveying 0.4 of a child, so we compromised by calling our smallest puppet "Point Four". Few other compromises were made. The family subsisted by eating and excreting money. All purchases were made by computer. All payments were made by the puppets with their right hands, which had usefully mutated into credit cards. These would be inserted into the slot provided by the computer. Nobody ever left home, because there was no reason to.

It was hardly Orwell or Huxley as a vision of the future, but we really enjoyed working out some of these ideas. Unfortunately, when we screened the thing it was really boring, all too ponderous and hopelessly overlong. I thought then that it highly unlikely that I would ever be able to do anything worthwhile with puppets.

When our time was up in Oregon, we moved to San Francisco, where I was confident I would find work on one of the newspapers. While Sophie galloped through our dwindling funds, riding the carousel in Golden Gate Park, I sussed out the employment prospects. I liked the gutsy approach of the *Bay Guardian*, but I found it was too poor to consider taking me on. The *San Francisco Chronicle* was rich enough but they thought my work was too highly seasoned for their readers' palates. They suggested I try the underground.

At first I thought they meant the subway, but they were only giving me a kindly steer to the underground press which served San Francisco's buoyant peace and love hippie community. I was not at all affronted by this suggestion, but I knew that such publications usually revolved around a little gang of mates, and I would have to develop contacts before I could get in. Meanwhile the money ran out. Deirdre and I decided that she and the children should return to England for the brief while that it would take for me to hit it big in America, and then they would come back. It would be another year before I would get to see them again.

The work, when I found it, was less exalted than sweeping the subway, but it had its compensations. I was taken on to draw what was known as the "Merch on the Fig" by an in-house fashion agency serving a big department store. No great initiative was required, all you had to do was draw the department store's merchandise on the human figures. And some of the figures were quite extraordinary. As this was San Francisco and I was in the fashion trade, it was naturally assumed that I was gay. So there would be this cavalcade of ladies, from blackest black to corn-fed white, taking off their clothes and putting on the "Merch", and vice versa, completely unselfconsciously in front of me. And I'd be trying to do the drawings while sweating bullets at the same time.

The stress of the work would be eased by the many opportunities for recreation in concerts at the Phillmore West and sometimes in the park. I would get to see the Grateful Dead, Jefferson Airplane and the wonderfully

The morning after.
Representatives of the Law
family, Sophie, Deirdre and
myself, introduce Peter Fluck to
the American West Coast. The
picture was taken on the porch
of our house in Portland,
Oregon, on the morning after
Fluck's welcoming party, a
punishing experience.
Right: Huey Newton, a leading
Black Panther on the California
scene, sitting comfortably with
assegai and rifle.

over-the-top Janis Joplin, who so took my fancy that I made a large-scale model of her. This was ultimately unsatisfactory because it could do no justice to her two greatest attributes - her voice, which was great, and her language, which was unbelievably foul.

My politics on the West Coast were catered for by the Peace and Freedom Party, a radical group which was closely allied to the Black Panthers. It was through this connection that I got to attend a number of Panther functions in Oakland, which were really quite extraordinary. When you went in, you would be given a joint as long as your arm and from then on it was all about having a ball. At one rally I remember they had a white tambourine girl with the band and she would periodically clap the instrument above her head in a motion that obliged her skirt to rise and reveal pure, all-American pussy. The outrageousness of the Panthers was probably the one issue on which all the policemen and all the feminists of America were totally united. Yet it was all curiously traditional in its way.

You realised that the macho attitude of the blacks was really their doing a kind of John Wayne, lone man with a gun, in reverse. It was Whitey who invented John Wayne and they were just turning the character around, though they could never bring themselves to dress badly enough to bring the masquerade off completely. There was, it's true, plenty to curdle the blood in the speeches, which usually consisted of graphic tales of wrongful arrest and shootouts with the police. But the ceremonies would invariably conclude on a note of uplift and sentiment. And the hard cases in shades with gun-holster bulges under their left armpits would respond with vigour to propositions like, "Can we now have a big hand for black American motherhood?"

On weekends I would spend lazy days in the park with new-found friends, working my way through a stack of joints. On one occasion I lamented the bother of having to roll them, and a friend told me it was possible to get the active ingredient of marijuana in pill form. Next time we were in the park, he produced the pills and the day flew magically by. Years later, when I returned to San Francisco and the same friend, I naturally asked him if he could still lay hands on supplies of the active ingredient of marijuana, and he told me not to be such a dumb Limey. We had tripped on LSD.

I would not tire of the sybaritic existence, but by the summer of 1968 it was evident that I was not about to find my fortune on the West Coast. I thought that perhaps it might be waiting for me in New York. Accordingly, I invested fifty dollars of my "Merch" money in a means of getting there, which proved to be a 1942 Dodge with a sawn-off broom handle holding the fan belt off the engine.

made the journey across America with a German-American friend from Reed College called Gary Achziger, and his girlfriend, Linda Burnham. Since I could not drive and Achziger was often too tired and emotional to drive, this placed a rather heavy burden on Linda. We would ease the problem by hitching hitchhikers. Anyone prepared to drive the decrepit heap for another hundred miles would be given a self-drive lift while Linda slept in the back. With these stratagems we crossed America at the speed of a wagon train, with frequent stops to observe the activities of the indigenous population.

In a populous place called Chicago we came across many men in blue beating up many youngsters in richly varied attire. We learned that the blue men were Major Daley's policemen, while the youngsters were demonstrators upset by the defeat of their cause at the Democratic National Convention, where the surviving peace candidate, Eugene McCarthy, had been outmanoeuvered by the old guard. The other peace candidate, called Robert Kennedy, had previously been shot. The young people, very naturally, were in a disillusioned frame of mind.

It was something of a lesson for me. Because my first experience of America had been confined to its more radical West Coast, I had tended to overestimate the forces of liberalism in the society. Chicago was a stern reminder of the existence of that other, more reactionary, America which was still very strong, and still in a very serious line of business.

We kept heading on east until we were rolling up Madison Avenue in New York, where the pavement-bound advertising executives looked at our vehicle with wild surprise. Some of the older ones, probably people who worked on the original Dodge account, broke into spontaneous applause. It was a fairy tale entry into a city, with a tragic sequel.

Unwise in the ways of the city, we parked the car illegally and the police, mistakenly thinking it was an abandoned vehicle, had it towed away. We then found that the 1942 Dodge had been reduced to a two by two feet metal cube.

In most other respects New York was good to me. I secured a commission from *Esquire* magazine in my first week, and I developed a connection with the Pushpin studio, a lively agency run by Seymour Chwast and Milton Glazer, who would soon start up *New York* magazine, and employ Julian Allen, a good friend of mine from art school, as its first artist reporter.

At night I would retreat to a cockroach-infested hole in the wall on the lower east side. At that stage I was trying to save every penny to bring my family over. This made me a rock-hard touch for the unfortunate Bowery Bums along my route home, though I would feel compelled to shell out for one who shuffled towards me with the line, "Have you got fifteen dollars for my ballet lessons?"

Towards the end of the year, David King came croaking back into my life. He had been sent over by the magazine to assemble illustrative material for an issue on America '68, a year that had been more eventful than most in that it contained two major political assassinations - of Robert Kennedy and Martin Luther King Jnr - no end of riots in the cities by disenchanted blacks, unrest on every campus, the deposing of a president by anti-war protesters, and was in the process of being topped off by an electoral choice between Richard Nixon and Hubert Humphrey, which seemed to provide powerful evidence for the survival of the unfittest.

We would discuss which items on this heavy menu he should select for the magazine but King also took a keen interest in my personal circumstances. On making his inspection of the lower east side he pronounced my living quarters totally unfit for human habitation. Then, out on the street, we saw one hobo leaning over another on the ground, solicitously we thought at first. Then it became apparent that the leaning hobo was carefully peeling off the fallen hobo's overcoat for his own personal use. King could then see that, by some New York standards, I had it made.

My main contribution to King's project was my most ambitious model to that date, featuring Chicago's Mayor Daley in command of a squad of blue-uniformed pigs. I also established that I had not entirely lost touch with events in Britain by fashioning another model of a desiccated Enoch Powell, as a British customs officer, poised menacingly over two naked black immigrants in an opened suitcase.

The New Year started brightly enough, but I needed to get my personal documentation in apple-pie order before bringing my family over. I had got into a tangle over my visa status but it was nothing serious, so I went to the downtown office of the visa people to straighten things out. I was interviewed there by a woman officer who seemed uncannily well clued up on my movements and contacts, including those with the Panthers and anti-war people in San Francisco. She was, not to put too fine a point on it, unsympathetic to my case. The way she saw it was, "We have enough trouble-makers like you here already, without importing any more."

To make matters worse I was asked to cite a reference, some person who could testify to my sterling personal qualities. I racked my brains to remember the last wholly respectable, bookish, middle-class character I had come across, and it was the father of Linda Burnham, the heroine of the cross-country drive. So I volunteered his name. It was only later that I discovered he was a leading member of the American Communist Party.

Through all this the Pushpin people were very supportive and helped me to get the best legal advice. The legal advice was that I could probably stay in America and successfully fight any deportation order if I was prepared to take on an expensive legal battle that would last for years, and during those years I would almost certainly have to remain separated from my family. The lawyer said that in his experience of similar cases very few marriages survived the course. But there was another way. If I made the life of the authorities much easier by voluntarily deporting myself, there was no reason why I should not be allowed to return after an interval of two years, with the slate wiped clean.

So I thought about the options, and I went quietly.

New York locations. Top left: David King, in *Midnight Cowboy* attire, outside the Chelsea Hotel. Bottom left: my spartan quarters on the lower east side. Above: me, at my most fragrant, outside the Chelsea Hotel after King let me use his bath.
Photographs: Left, Roger Law; Above, David King.

Overleaf: my model of Mayor Daley and the pigs, made at the Pushpin studio in New York, which appeared in the *Sunday Times*. I take only minor credit for the pigs' heads. They are, with the exception of the glass eyes, the real thing.
Photograph: Irving Schild

INTELLIGENT HOUSES 'In Chicago, Mayor Daley released unattractive and violent nature, created a police state and scenes that might have come from some brutal civil war' Elizabeth Hardwick, see page 34. Model by Roger Law

Chapter 7 I came back to England to

lick my American wounds,

and to a new, but thoroughly familiar, home.

While I had been in the United States, Deirdre

had made a strategic retreat with the children from

London to Cambridge, where they were now resident

in a tiny house in Orchard Street, near the city centre.

Model Behavio

Wearing your art on your sleeve

By Valerie Wade, photographs by Hans Feurer
If you are fed up with wearing the
results of anonymous mass-production
and want to buy something that needs
a certain amount of skill and originality
to make, then look out for fabrics
and clothes that have been printed,
painted or silk-screened by hand,
like the glossy velvet on this page and
everything on the next.
Left: shirt specially made by Liberty's
from French hand-painted panne
velvet that costs £7 10s a yard from
Liberty's, Regent Street, London W1.
Cover: silk blouse designed and
painted by Lyn and Mary. It costs 30gns
and can be ordered in any
size or colour. From Deborah & Clare,
29 Beauchamp Place, SW3

Modeller as male model: my heavy-lidded, homecoming appearance after America was deemed well suited to the promotion of a psychedelic creation on the *Sunday Times* fashion page.

It was familiar because my father had bought it ten years earlier for £500. It was part of a terrace scheduled for demolition but it had provided Deirdre and myself with a marital home in the few months before we bunked off to London. While we were away enjoying the delights of metropolitan society, the house had suffered from neglect and regular visits by vandals, but it had miraculously escaped demolition. Some alert architect, moved by the rare quality of the mansard roofs, had managed to ensure the preservation of the whole terrace. It still stands to this day.

Interestingly enough, all the major emporia in which I worked, like the *Observer* building in Tudor Street, the *Sunday Times'* headquarters in Gray's Inn Road, and the first Spitting Image factory in Canary Wharf, have all been razed utterly to the ground. I feel there is a moral in this somewhere, but I'm not sure what it is.

While I had been away Deirdre had fixed up the place, supplemented the family finances by doing magazine illustration, and preserved our two children, somewhat enlarged, but wholly intact. I could tell that I had some catching up to do on the bread-winning and parenting fronts. The trouble was that I felt so lethargic.

Back at the *Sunday Times* there was also a reassuring familiarity. Godfrey Smith still benignly surveyed the troops across his serene desk, Francis Wyndham and Michael Rand still sparked off the big ideas, and David King was still his unmistakable self. My first project for him, which we had discussed earlier in New York, was a model called "The Assassins", which focused on Lee Harvey Oswald, Sirhan Sirhan and James Earl Ray, the men who, reportedly at least, had bumped off John Kennedy, Robert Kennedy and Martin Luther King Jnr respectively. I did it with a lot of tomato ketchup and with a Stars and Bars background after the style of Jasper Johns, an American artist whom I very much admired. And I was pleased with it, but the work was oddly tiring.

I also had another project on the go about biological engineering, for which I had to construct a reasonably convincing womb and foetus. I made the foetus out of plasticine and the placenta out of a bathroom sponge. I painted them and left them propped up in the art department to dry overnight, and the early morning cleaners went through the roof. There had been some complaints before about my model-making materials adhering to cherished surfaces, but now it was showdown time. Smith called me in and said there was only one solution to the problem as far as he could see: in future I would have to do the model-making side of my work from home, and this would be written into my contract. This punishment was like music to my ears, as I was now very tired indeed.

All the same, I had to go up to London to work on more conventional

With my daughter Sophie, aged nine, in the garden of our house in Orchard Street, Cambridge.
Photograph: Deirdre Amsden

illustration projects and there was one very big one in the works. While the men and women of Insight specialised in investigations in depth, the magazine was more noted for what was known as investigations in width, some of which spanned several issues. And Godfrey Smith had come up with the widest one so far conceived - "The 1,000 Makers of the Twentieth Century". David King and I were to set to work on the design and illustrations. Before we could get to H for Hitler, I keeled over.

The diagnosis was hepatitis. I had it for almost a year and my main memory is of continuously trying to read the same page of a book and continuously giving up. I would lie all day on what Peter Fluck named "the Cosmic Couch", the sofa in the front room. Very occasionally I would make heavy-limbed expeditions to the Fitzwilliam Museum to give my eyes something to do. On an approved diet of white meat, nuts and lettuce there was not much pleasure to be had in eating. Drinking was out of the question, and I couldn't even smoke dope as it had the effect of making me itch all over. Not only was I incapable of doing anything, I thought I never would be capable of doing anything again. My loss of confidence was total.

After what seemed like an eternity, I began to pick up a little in the summer of 1970 when we spent several weeks in Minorca at a villa presciently acquired by my father with Littleport construction industry profits. The combination of sun, swimming and eating a more edible class of white meat was

When I lived in America violence seemed to be a lot more characteristic of the society than apple pie. The assassinations of Robert Kennedy and Martin Luther Jnr, both of which occurred during my stay, changed the direction of American politics just as much as the assassination of President John F. Kennedy had five years earlier. In all cases very much for the worse.

When David King came over to New York towards the end of 1968, we decided to try to tackle the subject of American political killings for the *Sunday Times* magazine. The model, right, was the result. Done after the style of the American artist Jasper Johns, each of the designated killers - Lee Harvey Oswald, James Earl Ray and Sirhan Sirhan - wears the campaigning button of his victim. The irony is that they also may have been victims. Over the years enough doubt has been shed to suggest that these three characters either were not the assassins or, if they were, they were no more than players of bit parts in larger conspiracies.

Photograph: David Montgomery

The African octopus: a photomontage composition which I devised to illustrate the grip of Johannes Vorster's white South Africa on a predominantly black continent. It appeared on the cover of the *Sunday Times* magazine in 1971 as part of its series on Planet Earth, one of the investigations in width that were much favoured in those days.

physically restoring but I was still a long way from being ready to commit myself to any form of work.

Eventually, Deirdre kicked me out. She could see that I had shaken off the hepatitis and that what I was ultimately suffering from was loss of bottle. So it was suitcases on the pavement time, and I was told to go to London and not to come back until I had managed to put some work together. In London I was received by Peter Fluck, not one of the world's prize-winning male nurses. But he very kindly allowed me to occupy the spare room in his flat, which also served as studio, off Kensington Church Street.

I could see from the evidence of industry in his studio that our roles had been reversed. Never one to overextend himself, Fluck used to accuse me of running around after too many commissions in order to satisfy a deep psychological need for overwork. Now it appeared to me that Fluck of all people might be prey to a similar condition. While I had been playing Rip Van Winkle, he kept the torch of model-making in Britain shining bright. Under the patronage of Alastair Burnet, the Editor of *The Economist*, he had been able to exhibit a series of notorious political specimens on the magazine's front cover. His study of Harold Wilson had been so evil-looking that Michael Heseltine had offered to buy it. Another of his regular customers, both for grotesques and illustrations, was the *Radio Times*. Beyond that Fluck produced a regular caricature for *Labour Weekly*, the abnormally unsuccessful, official party publication. Fluck told me that he liked to do it as it gave him the opportunity to practise caricature in print and in complete privacy.

Oppressed by all this work in the home, I fled to the *Sunday Times*, where David King was ready to put me on the lightest of light duties. And Deirdre was right, it was just my nerve that had gone. Within a few days back at the newspaper I knew I would be equal to anything they could throw at me. Some weeks later, around the beginning of 1971, I was allowed back into the marital home.

Deirdre had always been a moderate person, neither smoking, nor drinking alcohol, nor eating meat. The only thing she liked to excess was me, on occasion. Now, in the wake of my illness and with what seemed like somebody else's metabolism, I too had to learn the art of moderation. This was perhaps overdue in my case, as my consumption of drink and drugs had probably been some way above the national average. My life changed quite radically. I became more regular in my habits and in the time I had once spent drinking, I would raise rabbits with Sophie and do all manner of wholesome things, but I would allow myself the occasional relapse.

One of these occurred on the publication of David King's photographic book about Leon Trotsky. We were both drunk and in a cheerful state of mind in the West End and I thought it would be a good time to teach my good friend a skill I had not exercised since my student days in Cambridge - how to walk on

THE SUNDAY TIMES *magazine*

OCTOBER 10

IVORY COAST

SOUTH AFRICA

KENYA

MALAWI

RHODESIA

TANZANIA

ZAMBIA

LESOTHO

PLANET EARTH 3:
Black Africa, White Africa

THE SUNDAY TIMES *magazine*

HAILSHAM
The man who sits on
the Woolsack

**These two versions of Lord
Hailsham, as Lord Chancellor
and knockabout clown, were
used to illustrate one of the long
profile articles written by Susan
Barnes, who was the wife of the
leading Labour politician Tony
Crosland. Her access to top politicians - in all parties - gave her
pieces an extra depth. I always
enjoyed illustrating them.**

Photograph: Brian Morris

the roofs of parked cars. Unfortunately, one of the cars was a cab, pulling away,
which led to my dislocating my ankle. This probably accounted for the leniency with which King and I were treated when we subsequently appeared before
Bow Street magistrates' court on drunk and disorderly charges.

King was a much more political animal than I could ever be, and he persuaded the *Sunday Times*, which was still Conservative in its editorial outlook,
to run a long succession of articles on Lenin, Trotsky and Chairman Mao and
other like-minded characters. In the course of this occupation he would amass
the finest collection of early revolutionary photographs outside the Iron Cur-
tain. It was the extraordinary pictures of course that made the subject matter
palatable to his less radical superior editors. King's other obsession, less controversial politically but not without its complications, was with the boxer Cassius
Clay, later known as Muhammed Ali.

Not long after my return to work, Godfrey Smith was moved to another
job to be replaced by a very young old Etonian called Magnus Linklater who,
from our point of view, was very much an unknown quantity. By way of breaking the new editor in to the ethos of the magazine King invited Linklater to
come along and watch an Ali v Joe Frazier fight, being screened live in a
Finsbury Park cinema at three o'clock in the morning. It was apparently a
scene of the utmost degradation, with an ankle-deep litter of beer cans and
broken peanut shells, and a din that could only be made by the best concentration of fighting drunks in London. As they were sitting down, Linklater said in
an upper-class *sotto voce* that pierced the atmosphere like a knife: "What an
interesting class of person we have here." For a few seconds the cinema went
awfully quiet. To this day King believes he owes his life to the fact that nobody
in the upper circle could actually believe their own ears.

Linklater, who now edits the *Scotsman*, became a wonderful editor of the
magazine. He was as liberal as Smith, but much more enthusiastic and, of
course, more of our own age. He was a cut above us in the class spectrum,
being the son of the novelist Eric Linklater with high connections in the
Scottish aristocracy, but as he went so thoroughly native, this never presented
any difficulty. The only pity was that he lasted only three years before Harry
Evans moved him on.

In that time I got to model most of the leading political figures of the day,
often as an accompaniment to long feature articles written by Susan Crosland
and Hugo Young. I still kept my hand in as a freelance, doing Ken Russell as
"Narcissus" for *Men Only* and Noël Coward for *Nova*, replete with a beautiful
set of butterfly wings which Deirdre designed and made out of a piece of
velene. In fact, most of my models' outfits were made by Deirdre in this period
which accounts for their unusually well turned out appearance.

There were frustrations of course. My study of Rupert Murdoch as a street
flasher, with a copy of the *Sun* obscuring his erogenous zone, was done at high

Circus politics. In the approach to the 1974 General Election the Liberal Party, led by Jeremy Thorpe, was seen as a threat to a majority by either the Tories, under Ted Heath, or Labour, led by Harold Wilson. Susan Barnes wrote a long article about the situation which I illustrated by having Thorpe pose the threat with custard pies on one page, and delivering it on the next.
Photograph: Brian Morris

speed to illustrate an article about the great newspaper proprietor written by Peter Dunn. It then got stuck in the works for eighteen months before Harry Evans, who had cravenly shown the material to Murdoch, felt he could allow it to appear. In the course of routine research for a feature on the House of Commons, Tom Driberg had shown King and I around the place and, as a bonus, detailed the various locations where he had pleasured himself with certain high-ranking persons. We passed the salient details on to Linklater, whose response was a model of rectitude. The magazine, he said, was no place for a cocksucker's guide to the House of Commons.

This was not quite Driberg's last hurrah but his health was deteriorating rapidly. He would retreat more and more often to his flat in the Barbican, where he would endlessly watch television with failing eyes, but with his instincts still wholly intact. I remember visiting him there once when a row of leggy dancing girls flashed up on the screen. Driberg peered and then turned to me and asked, "Are they really boys?" It seemed an innocent enough lie to say that they really were.

My great pleasure at this time was going back to the United States. My own misbehaviour in relation to that country had long since dwindled into insignificance. The only misbehaviour that Americans were seriously interested in now was that of their own government. The spectacle of Richard Nixon, always a caricaturist's prime target on account of his ski-jump nose, being dragged down by the Watergate crisis was hardly edifying but it had to be classed as compelling drama. The crisis would create a tremendous appetite for Americana in Europe and I was happy to bring in relief supplies in the form of effigies of bent politicians and bloated capitalists.

On these American journeys I was able to colour in some of the blanks left from my first grand tour. I penetrated the Catskill mountains, where I met Clarence Schmidt, a quintessential American loony genius, dedicated to the improvement of nature. His specialisms were mountain-painting and tree-rearrangement. He would strip down the branches, wrap them in aluminium foil, and then reattach them to the trees to form superior designs. They were certainly most striking. Schmidt told me that in the little time he had to spare, he was rewriting the Bible.

I met a more ominous species of nutter in Winnfield, Louisiana, the home town of Huey Long, the South's most notorious political son. "How long you bin in this country, boy?" the sheriff asked me. Two months, I confessed. "Goddam," he said. "You speak pretty good American." By day there was an almost tangible racial tension about the place, but by ten o'clock in the evening it was asleep, not unlike Littleport in that respect. A local reporter asked me what I thought about the place, obviously inviting me to drop myself in it with some smart-ass liberal remark, but I spoke the simple truth. I said it reminded me of home.

Joint administration. In its early days the National Theatre was administered by Laurence Olivier, once the world's greatest actor, with Kenneth Tynan, once the world's most acerbic theatre critic. They did not get along famously well. For an article in the *Sunday Times* magazine about problems at the National, I modelled Olivier as Richard III with his greatest affliction - the humpback - in the form of the loquacious Tynan.
Overleaf: Richard Seifert, London's greatest high-rise architect, as Centrepoint.
Photographs: Brian Morris

SEIFERT ON OUR SKYLINE

Richard Seifert has done more to change the face of London than any architect since Sir Christopher Wren – and some would even argue that Seifert's buildings have had, and will have, more impact on the capital than St Paul's or the famous Wren churches. The hundred-yard high Centre Point tower at the bottom of Tottenham Court Road is Richard Seifert's most striking construction to date, but even that giant will be dwarfed in a year or so by the 600ft. skyscraper planned

High jinks

Richard Seifert's Centre Point building was highly controversial in the early 1970s, and has its critics to this day. But it was undeniably distinctive, and it made an even more distinctive, if highly unattractive, suit.

The Seifert model was more complicated than most in that it involved a mix of photographic, photomontage and modelling techniques. The photograph of the building, right, and the model, above right, were the two main elements that had to be combined, above left.

I also felt there should be another component to the model, namely money, raining down from the heavens. As the man who could squeeze most office footage into the smallest space, Seifert's services were prized by the richest developers. But the feeling was that the model had already scaled a sufficient height and that any reference to mony would be over the top.

Photograph: Brian Morris

Rupert Murdoch as a Mac Flasher. This was assembled, like the Seifert model, by a combination of modelling and photomontage techniques. The background in this image is Bouverie Street, just off Fleet Street, where the *Sun* was located before Murdoch moved his newspaper operation to Wapping. The Flasher did not take long to construct but it took eighteen months before the *Sunday Times* decided that it could be published. It was eventually run in the magazine as illustration for a profile of Murdoch by Peter Dunn.

I always considered Murdoch one of the targets most worthy of caricature, not through any deficiency in his features, but because of what seemed to me the almost contemptuous way in which he managed to manipulate British newspapers and, through them, British society. Later, at Spitting Image, we would do a model of a lookalike Murdoch pissing an England-shaped puddle. Later still we would... but we'll come to that later in this book.

Photograph: Brian Morris

THE PRESIDENT last January—confident and ebullient as he announced the Vietnam ceasefire agreement. The Watergate storm had yet to break.

L'Impudique Albion

Kicking Richard Nixon around

Richard Nixon suffered more at the hands of caricaturists than most political leaders. This was partly because his foxy features gave them the most tremendous scope, and partly because these features did not lie. I would put him in the Harold Wilson class as someone it was politically correct to dislike purely on the grounds of his face. He was also marked as a target because of his famous "Goodbye" to the press - "You won't have Richard Nixon to kick around any more" - uttered when announcing a retirement from politics that proved to be wholly temporary.

When the Watergate crisis broke, every cartoonist around the planet felt the need to pull out a few extra stops. Their task was not made any easier by the physical changes in their old adversary. As he stumbled down the path to disgrace and eventually resignation from the office of President of the United States, Nixon's features reorganised themselves, above left, from those of a crafty huckster to a resemblance of Captain Queeg. At about this time Tony Hendra, one of the editors of *National Lampoon* in Washington, asked me to do a Nixon. There was no specific brief but the preference was for something as gross as possible.

For personal inspiration I turned to one of the 1905 issues of *L'Assiette au Beurre*, above right, and Jean Veber's representation of "Perfidious Albion" featuring Edward VII as Britannia's exposed backside. It then took only a tiny leap of the imagination to produce my model, right, of Richard Nixon as Uncle Sam's exposed, and flatulent, rear.

Photograph: Brian Morris

A model form of relaxation: poking my nose into other people's business

The new look: to commemorate 1975 I art-directed an issue with original paintings of the year's most newsworthy characters, but not in the guises you might expect. Thus Idi Amin graced the cover Annigoni-style (actually by Michael Leonard) and inside, John Stonehouse appeared as discarded togs beside a David Hockney-style swimming pool.

The artist as reporter: as a break from modelling grotesques I would sometimes be allowed to research and write stories of my own. My main achievement in this area was a full-length study of Arno Brecker, Hitler's favourite sculptor, right. But my most exciting assignment was covering the Portuguese revolution and the fall of Salazar, far right, which I did in conjunction with the writer Alex Mitchell.

PLUS: PLANET EARTH 7-NORTH AMERICA

Portugal's secret police and the revolution which unmasked them

Scoops: on the old *Sunday Times* everybody (not excepting illustrators) was encouraged to bring in original stories. Two of mine that featured on the cover were a find of George Grosz's last photomontages, and how to crack supermarket codes, an item I first discovered lurking in the columns of the *San Francisco Bay Guardian*.

The code on this chocolate cake pack is its 'death' date. After that, the makers stipulate, it must not be sold. But six days later we were still able to buy it See page 12 and find out

there was one aspect of life on the *Sunday Times* which Smith tolerated, and Linklater positively encouraged, that very much appealed to me. This could be defined as doing somebody else's thing. I rarely felt trapped in my role as illustrator or model-maker because, if the inclination took me, I could branch out as a photographer, a story tipster, a picture researcher, a writer's researcher, or even a writer.

One of my first assignments in this area involved working with Colin Simpson, an ace Insight investigator with a British army background. My task was only vaguely defined but it appeared that my main duty would be to act as a back-up witness to his investigations, while taking a few photographs as reference for the colour drawings I was to prepare. Our mission was to look into the affairs of a shady bank in Morocco and we met by pre-arrangement in Gibraltar.

My first surprise in Gibraltar was the discovery of another back-up witness, Simpson's pretty young bride of very recent vintage. So we were honeymooning and investigating at the same time. Stealth was apparently of the essence, as the approach to Morocco was made in a small boat of dubious seaworthiness which Simpson had hired at the quayside. Within twenty minutes of setting foot on Moroccan soil we were all under arrest.

Simpson remonstrated with the cops in best British gunboat commander style, but they were unmoved. It appeared that the coastguards had given

News-Photo Team Here
London Times Doing Story On Earl, Huey

Roger Law, features editor from Cambridge, England, and Ede Rothaus, lady photographer from New York, are in Winnfield this week doing research on the Longs, Earl and Huey, for a story to be published in the London Times.

The story is part of their assignment to gather material on great families in the U.S.

They are the second metropolitan news team to come here on a "Long" assignment in recent months. The New York Times published a story about Huey Long and Winn Parish a few weeks ago.

"Winnfield is pretty much like home," Law said. Everything closes at 10."

He said that he has been treated fantastically well and he has no complaints.

"The Longs are by far the most interesting subject," Law observed. "The story has to do with people."

"We are researching the story now and it will be written by a Southerner. He will be a top-flight writer," Law explained.

Law attended Cambridge School of Art. His profession is illustrating magazines and he is a reporter for the London Times. Ede Rothaus is a New York photographer working on contract.

The story should come out in the fall in the London Sunday Times Magazine, Law said.

Sowers. 3. Report of Poppy sale, 4. Girls state 5. members discussed some possible Bicentennial project

This research team, Ede Rothaus, New York photographer, and Roger Law, London reporter, are in Winn Parish information about the famous Long family.

Making the news: in small-town America, especially below the Mason-Dixon line, inquisitive outsiders are themselves subjected to inquisition. In the story, above Ede Rothaus, a New York photographer, and I are put through the wringer by the Winnfield *Enterprise-News-American*. I think we conducted ourselves rather well.

them concrete intelligence of the arrival of a smuggler's vessel with a description of the three people on board that fitted us almost perfectly - one white man, one white woman and one Japanese sumo wrestler. After Simpson had been allowed to place a number of furious phone calls, which must have alerted the rest of North Africa to the arrival of the undercover investigative team, the police started to relent. And when the boat proved to be "clean", it was convivial mint teas all round.

The honeymoon-cum-investigation was then allowed to proceed in orderly fashion on to Casablanca, Marrakesh and Fez, though the bank story always proved elusive. Apparently unfazed, Simpson dug up two alternative stories - one about gun-running and the other about missing art treasures - to appease his masters back home, and rounded off a memorable trip by giving me an advance class in how to do my expenses.

I had a different kind of education from Murray Sayle, with whom I became closely acquainted during one of the magazine's investigations in width. This particular one involved saturation coverage of a day in the life of Cambridge, and due to a logistical cock-up we found ourselves both doing the night shift observing Newnham College for any sign of newsworthy activity. As there was not a lot to report, Sayle gave me the benefits of his wit and wisdom. He was the oldest of a lively tribe of Australians on the *Sunday Times* and he took his responsibilities as an elder seriously.

Journalism was, he said, essentially about stereotypes but it was a bad idea to get stuck with the same ones. He gave Insight, to which he had been a major contributor, as a for instance. Originally it had been based on the twin propositions: "We name the guilty man. Arrow points to defective part." But

Left: interviewing Clarence Schmidt, the Catskill mountain artist, in the old people's home to which he had been moved after his tree-house burned down. Above: examples of Schimdt's work in a mountain hut window. My friend Julian Allen, of *New York* magazine, fills in the broken panes.
Photograph: Roger Law

Nature imitates caricature. I did this model of Peter Walker, top, the Tory Cabinet Minister, as a song and dance man for *Nova* magazine. Very shortly afterwards he appeared in a newspaper photograph, above, as the spitting image of his caricature. Right: *Nova* also asked me to model the great fixer, Lord Goodman, seen here extracting a plum from a pie, but this image was never used. Presumably they were frightened it might have a similar effect.

Photographs: Brian Morris

the genre had become debased by overuse and poor imitation. What was needed now was a new, more big-hearted stereotype. He was not sure what it should be but one he was thinking of trying for size was "We name the innocent man." Though Sayle was one of the best writing journalists on the paper, he never, unlike some lesser writers, implied there was some great mystique about his activity. The only qualities necessary for a journalist were, he said, "rat-like cunning, a plausible manner, and a little literary ability".

I knew I would never master a plausible manner but my encounters with Sayle encouraged me to exercise what little literary ability I had, and I would eventually assemble a long article about Arno Brecker, Hitler's favourite sculptor, words and pictures, which ran in the magazine.

My scoops included a find of George Grosz's last photomontages in Manhattan, which appeared in the magazine with a selection of his previously unpublished letters. I was also a seminal influence on the inquiry into supermarket codes, which effectively concealed the antiquity of the food people bought in the shops. This latter achievement led to debates in the Commons, a change in the law and crusading appearances on television by Harry Evans. Now it can be revealed that the story was first written in the *San Francisco Bay Guardian* and clipped out and brought back to inspire a British version by the *Sunday Times'* itinerant model-maker.

My scoop that got away was a marvellous collection of *fin de siècle* drawings and erotica by Miklos Vadash, who had been one of the leading illustrators on *L'Assiette au Beurre*. They belonged to an elderly relative of Vadash who lived in St John's Wood and whom I would occasionally visit. I once took Paul Hogarth along and he thought the material was "almost as good as Lautrec". I had hoped to get some of it in the magazine but the old man could never bring himself to release it. After his death I heard that a lot of the stuff had found its way into the collection of Victor Lowndes, the *Playboy* supremo.

The most exciting assignment for me was covering the Portuguese revolution and the fall of Salazar. I did this in conjunction with Alex Mitchell, another spirited Australian, who provided me with a list of contacts and wrote up the dispatches I sent back from Lisbon. I went around collecting secret police files which had been scattered in the streets and generally hoovering up an incredible atmosphere. At one point I saw a mass of fired-up sailors and soldiers issuing from a cinema. I looked up at the hoarding to see what was so exciting and they were showing Eisenstein's *Battleship Potemkin*. My main task was picking up pictures and statements from people who had been tortured by the Salazar regime. These were not in short supply.

There were some hard left journalists on the *Sunday Times*, though many fewer than Rupert Murdoch liked to imagine. But for the most part they were talkers, rather than doers. Alex Mitchell was an exception. Though a very good writer he took a major salary cut to work on *Ink*, a short-lived revolutionary

Revolutionary Art. The cartoon, above, was crafted for one of the early issues of _Ink_, one of the more flagrantly combative newspapers of its day. It had to be an early issue, as funds would run out before we could do any later ones. The character on strings, right, is my way of demonstrating the flexibility of Harold Wilson. _Nova_ ran his gyrations over several pages. This is the first one.

Photographs: John Claridge

publication, and an even bigger one to become Editor of _Newsline_, the official newspaper of Gerry Healy's Trotskyite Workers' Revolutionary Party which, like most such parties, ended in tears.

Many of Mitchell's old mates on the _Sunday Times_ would go on about the waste of his talent, but I never looked at it in that light. I could not bring myself to join any political party, partly on the Groucho Marxist principle that I should not belong to any organisation that was willing to have me, but mainly because I knew I was congenitally incapable of toeing the party line. But I was also very grateful for the existence of the parties of the far left, and I would readily supply _Ink_ and _Newsline_ and other similar organs with low-cost cartoons and caricatures.

It seemed to me then, and to some extent now, that they were the only agencies through which working-class people could get an education in what capitalism was all about. Unfortunately, they had no talent whatsoever for telling people what Communism was all about.

'A second devaluation would be regarded all over the world as an acknowledgement of defeat' (July 1961)

'This party is a moral crusade or it is nothing' (Sept 1962)

'One export will fall sharply under a Labour Government—the export of British scientists' (Jan 1964)

'I, unlike Canute, have waited until high tide before giving my command' (April 1965)

'Next year we hope to finish the job completely' (April 1965)

'The brain drain is due to the deficiency of the British industrial system' (Oct 1967)

'The economy is now showing signs of moving upwards' (Nov 16 1964)

'Devaluation is a tremendous opportunity for exporters' (Nov 19 1967)

The image of Noël Coward, below, sucking honey out of a flower was made to accompany a tribute to him which appeared in *Nova* magazine. It can readily be seen that the artistry in this creation is not so much in the modelling but in the dress and, of course, the exquisite butterfly wings. Most of my models in this period were dressed by Deirdre Amsden, but making Noël Coward's wings - fashioned out of velene - was perhaps her finest hour.

The long-domed Lord Longford naturally excited caricaturists when he took up anti-pornography campaigning in a big way. I did this study of a Longford lookalike, right, assessing the corrupting potential of a skin mag, for *Nova* magazine. Unhappily, my educational study of the demoralising effect of the skin mag on the model, far right, proved surplus to the magazine's requirements.

Photographs: Brian Morris

They're Off. This study of
Princess Anne and Captain Mark
Phillips, another mix of
photomontage and modelling,
was made for *Nova* magazine on
the occasion of their marriage. I
came quite late to the royals,
and then really only as a result of
a request. This particular model
was commissioned by David
Hillman, a friend of mine at the
Sunday Times, who had moved
on to become art editor of *Nova*.
Later on, as the Fluck and Law
partnership evolved into Spitting
Image, the royals became a
much bigger item. And we would
be fiercely criticised, by Mrs
Whitehouse among others, for
making mockery of people who
could not answer back. My own
feeling is that the royals'
"inability to answer back" is
clearly a matter of their own
choice and certainly not a fact of
life. Moreover, as mockery of the
Royal Family goes, ours is mild in
comparison to much that has
gone before. People who are
keen to know just how savage
anti-royal caricature can be
should consult James Gillray's
studies of George IV. In those
days the Crown exhibited a
healthy ability to answer back
by buying up Gillray's plates. So
far, alas, I have yet to be
tempted with a similar offer for
the models.

Photograph: Brian Morris

Luck and

Flaw

I remember one time, in the later 1970s, being summoned to the editor's office, where Harry Evans seemed to have something on his mind. He asked me what I was doing exactly. So I told him about some of the more interesting things, like making model caricatures for the New York Times and Der Spiegel, and about the plans I had to bring out an illustrated version of Charles Dickens' A Christmas Carol for Penguin Books. And I was just about to tell him about the new line in ceramic caricature mugs I was exploring, when I saw the great editor's eyes were glazing over. "No," he said. "I meant, what are you doing for us?"

Photograph: John Lawrence Jones

he answer was not a lot. Whereas once I had done about eighty per cent of my work for the *Sunday Times* with the other twenty per cent freelance, these proportions had now effectively been reversed. This situation had not come about by accident.

People who once worked for the *Sunday Times* invariably have their own date for when things ceased to be as they used to be, usually with the implication that any change was for the worse. A popular date for moaners of this type is 1983, when the rough-hewn Andrew Neil arrived as editor and vigorously set about dispersing the last tribes of Harold Evans. More popular still is 1981, when Rupert Murdoch first took over as proprietor and began to stamp his unique imprint on the newspaper. Some others make a good case for 1978, when the combined stupidity of the pre-Murdoch management and the print unions succeeded in keeping the paper off the streets for a whole year. I personally, however, would date my own moan from late 1974, when the advertising and marketing departments first seriously got their grappling hooks into the magazine.

By that time the *Sunday Times* magazine had long since lost the novelty value of being first and was in fierce competition with the *Observer* and *Telegraph*, and later with many others, for colour advertising revenue. The way ahead, the advertising people thought, was to make the magazine much more consumer-oriented, essentially making the editorial content serve their perception of the needs of the market. Magnus Linklater thought this was a really lousy idea, and said so. Within a few months he was summarily relieved of his command, and replaced by Hunter Davies, who took to the journalism of how to mow your lawn, how to buy your car and how to brush your dog's teeth, like a duck to water.

Davies was a capable writer and a clever man, but his horizon tended to be somewhat limited. He was fond of saying that anything worth doing could be done between the hours of nine and five which could conceivably be true for a Cumbrian bank clerk but did not seem to accord with the experience of any creative people I had come across. Matters beyond Dover were of modest interest and even the ideas on the home front tended be treated warily unless they were sanctified by being in the current news, or signposted by PR blurbs. The old magazine's emphasis on trying to break original stories, on the "You saw it here first" principle, inevitably took more of a back seat.

The advertisers had always been inclined to kick up when their products appeared in issues featuring Don McCullin's searing war pictures. For a while they had nothing to worry about as Davies would have the world's greatest war photographer taking snaps of Hadrian's Wall and Consett in County Durham. McCullin's great talent would soon be re-engaged, but my skills, and those of David King could not so readily find a place. King was accustomed to a tremendous flexibility when laying out the magazine, but the adverts were now phased through the magazine in a way that broke up most of the best spreads. This was no impediment to the little wordbite stories that were the order of the day, but it was the enemy of any grand design. It goes without saying that caricature models were not a highly prized item. Michael Rand was shifted to the newspaper shortly after Linklater's departure and replaced by Edwin Taylor, a designer more attuned to the requirements of the new regime. As he went, Rand said to King and myself, "Boys, the party's over." But he didn't have to tell us.

There was never any major row. I simply stopped volunteering ideas, and very few were offered to me. My contribution to the magazine, like those of David King and Francis Wyndham, simply withered away. And eventually I was let go. Though it was on offer, I did not take any redundancy money because I reckoned I must have got that before I left.

I had invested some of my unearned income from the *Sunday Times* in a place of worship. This was a small Methodist Temperance chapel, though in latter days an abandoned monument to dry rot, which I bought for £1,500 and was located only a few hundred yards from our home in Orchard Street. Deirdre, like the *Sunday Times* before her, had expressed enthusiasm to have my model-making done at some other address and the chapel was it.

As my freelance activity expanded, principally through contacts in the United States, I invited Deirdre to share the load of work in a formal business partnership. She responded to this opportunity by saying that it was perhaps the worst idea I had had in my life, and that I should know that being married to me was quite bad enough without any further association. I was therefore obliged to be extremely nice to Peter Fluck.

We already had a name for a partnership, Luck and Flaw. It had been bestowed on us back in our college days by Alec Heath, the head of the art school, as he was changing his trousers. Our tutors were always changing their trousers in those days before rushing off to be seen at some smart university event. On one such occasion a young member of staff had burst in on Heath,

Aspects of the demon drink. Above: a caricature of me by Richard Yeend. Left: the abandoned Temperance chapel in Cambridge that provided a workshop for Luck and Flaw, a home for Henry Kissinger's model, and a doorpost to lean on for our photographer John Lawrence Jones. Below: an ancient handwritten message found in a bottle behind the chapel's commemoration stone.

The United States was the first serious overseas market for the joint productions of Peter Fluck and myself. In general the Americans liked their models to be bigger and more brash than those we made for British publications, although there were limits. Our model entitled "Hubert Humphrey pulls it off", bottom left, was rejected even by the satirical *National Lampoon*. But Henry Kissinger sacrilegiously posing as the Statue of Liberty, bottom right, found favour with the *New York Times* and, later, *The Economist*. Our studies of George Wallace, the crippled Segregationist candidate in the 1976 presidential election, appeared in the *New York Times*, above right, and, mildly adapted, in the *Sunday Times*, above left. The *New York Times* rejected our idea of having Wallace running for office on his hands as being too cruel, though it seemed less cruel than the policies he was advocating.

Photographs: Bob Cramp

Overleaf: early glimpses of two of our most enduring characters. Reagan emerges from a cowboy boot, guns blazing, to contest the 1976 election, unsuccessfully on that occasion. Mrs Thatcher, as the new Prime Minister, is portrayed as an Iron Maiden for the *Sunday Times*.

Photographs: John Lawrence Jones

trousers round ankles, who looked up and said: "For God sake close the door, before that awful pair Luck and Flaw see me like this." And the spoonerism had stuck.

The first big job we did together was a series of models featuring the candidates running in the 1976 presidential election. This was interesting because when the *New York Times* first commissioned me to do the work, they insisted on my going down to Washington and making the acquaintance of my political victims. I had never been all that keen on seeing the people I caricatured in case they exhibited some redeeming qualities which could only spoil my aim. But as it was part of the commission I did as requested, and I was escorted round the offices of a variety of Senators by Ruth Ancel, the newspaper's art director, and introduced as "the illustrator" for the paper's election coverage.

It did not spoil my aim to any marked degree. In the case of Hubert Humphrey, the archetype of the flesh-pressing, glad-handing politician, I was unable to spot any redeeming features. I did not take to Edward Kennedy very much either, despite our common feature - the tell-tale red rings round the end of the nose that denote a long-term fondness for booze. But Kennedy at least was smart. Of all the politicians I saw, he was the only one who asked what my illustrations consisted of. "Ah," he grunted, when I explained. "So you're the hangman." There was, however, one aspect of this itinerary that was slightly disturbing - the politician I found far and away the most likeable was Barry Goldwater, the standard bearer of the extreme right.

The *New York Times* work was good, high profile stuff for the partnership but there were limits to what we could do. Fluck and I had the idea of doing George Wallace, the crippled Segregationist candidate, emerging from his wheelchair and racing away on his hands, over the caption, "Up and running". This was deemed some way beyond the limits. No such constraint was necessary when we worked for *National Lampoon*, the Washington-based satirical magazine, where our contact editor was Tony Hendra, who had once strutted the boards in Cambridge Footlights with John Cleese.

At our first meeting Hendra asked me if I would consider doing a model of Mel Brooks in chopped chicken liver. I knew then that we were on the same wavelength. Hendra gave us a king-size order for a series of ten models, each representing a different country in what was to be called the United States of Europe. They were all published in great style, except Italy, which was in no way untypical of the rest featuring, as it did, an Italian Euro-soldier behaving in a cowardly and sexually rampant manner. So why not Italy? "Do you want two pairs of broken legs?" asked Hendra. "Who do you think distributes this goddam paper?"

Fluck and I would settle down in the chapel, producing models at a steady clip of forty a year, about three of which we thought were reasonably good. Like all couples forced into extreme intimacy, we became odd, with our own

CENSORED
We have been told that we can't show the prick on this page (but we've shown him anyway).

Shoot-out in New Hampshire

individual curmudgeonly ways. Fluck would disguise his envy of my ability as a salesman of grotesque ideas by saying that I only got orders by threatening to kill people, which was largely untrue. I would mask my resentment of Fluck's superior ingenuity by saying that the only reason he thought laterally was because he was too lazy to think like any normal human being, which was largely true.

When some crucial deadline approached, I used to watch Fluck out of the corner of my eye with appalled fascination. He would drop some vital tool off the bench, but instead of picking it up like anybody else, he would set to work making a replacement tool from the odds and sods on the bench. If I dared to say anything, he would fudge the issue with a crafty remark like, "It's too hot to bend down." As a matter of fact, during the summer months, it was too hot in all positions. We had no end of experts coming to counsel us on how to improve the ventilation in the chapel but the best advice, given by a highly qualified architect, was that we should wear kaftans.

I never doubted my partner's ability, but I would have occasional paranoid worries about his ability to exercise his ability. These worries came over me once when I was in Addenbrooke's hospital with a suspected kidney complaint. As it happened, my brother Martin, who has a similar configuration to my own, was visiting me at the time and he very generously consented to occupy my bed while I went round to the chapel to check up on Fluck's activity level. I need not have worried. Fluck was working away as good as gold. But it proved to be an alarming day for Martin. When I crept back to the hospital I

THE SUNDAY TIMES *magazine*

COMING SOON:
THE UNITED STATES OF EUROPE

The United States of Europe feature ran in most European countries, see cover for *Sunday Times* version, left, as well as in the *National Lampoon*, but with some interesting variations. Most publications ran the series in full, but excluded the caricature of their own country. This suggested that, while similar prejudices about different nationalities are widely shared, there is a profound sensitivity about being on the receiving end of such prejudice.

Our original Euro-soldier, top left, was a sexually rampant Italian in full flight from battle after the nearest girl. It was not published in America, as it was thought the Mafia might not be amused. We made, top right, a less priapic model for Europe. We also, as we thought, toned down Germany as Euro-cop, bottom left and right, by removing the gore, but only succeeded in making the image more ominous.

Photographs: John Lawrence Jones

found that he had been given my routine test for blood pressure, and it had proved higher than the previous level recorded by his sick brother.

The yin and yang of the Luck and Flaw partnership consisted essentially of me thinking up undoable ideas, and Fluck figuring out ways of doing them, if only to spite me. His most superlative achievement was working out how to make twenty-six caricatures dance for Mr Fezziwig's Ball in our version of *A Christmas Carol*, though his creation of a vomit-gun to demonstrate the effects of English cuisine on a fastidious palate was a very close runner-up. Fluck was also responsible for the credible modelling of life-size hands, which led to one of the great leaps forward in our work.

In the early days all our models were relatively small, with big heads and little bodies. Inevitably, each model would have to have its own little made-to-measure outfit. Although Fluck took over from Deirdre as the dresser to the models it was evident, even to me, that the task was a bit on the thankless side. The reason for this was that the real end product of our work was not so much the model itself but the photograph of it, the transparency which would be used by the magazines and newspapers. Once we had a character photographed we scrunched him up and used the plasticine to make another one. Its exquisitely crafted little togs would be just thrown away or used to muck out the chapel sink. I knew that Deirdre found the disposable aspect of the work highly repellent, and Fluck was none to keen on it either.

The answer, of course, was to go life-size with the models, which would give them the choice of a vast range of classy gear from jumble sales and Oxfam. Going life-size would also spare us the problem of miniaturising all the props. Instead of wielding little wooden axes, they could wield real axes. But we did not go life-size for a long time, mainly because we could never make hands that did not look like a bunch of bananas. But Fluck cracked it in the end, and vastly extended our range.

One of the arts of the model caricaturist is the art of compromise. Our more staid customers, like the *New York Times*, the *Sunday Times* and *The Economist*, rarely gave a totally free reign to the Luck and Flaw partnership. To a large extent our images would have to be negotiated, and we would wind up with what we could get away with rather than what we originally intended. If we wanted to do something really outrageous, we tended to seek out more rarefied publications, like *National Lampoon* in the United States and *Men Only* in Britain. We felt that the election of a Tory government in 1979 and the emergence of Britain's first woman Prime Minister called for something outrageous. We therefore persuaded *Men Only* to run models of the new Tory Cabinet in various stages of undress. Top left: Willie Whitelaw, as an unclothed jailer, in celebration of the new "short, sharp shock" prison regime. Below left: Geoffrey Howe, fiddling while London burned down. Below right: Keith Joseph, one of Mrs Thatcher's early guru figures, as a nude vampire. Opposite: Mrs Thatcher as "Miss Discipline".

Photographs: John Lawrence Jones

Bovver Boys. Our model of Norman Tebbit, left, as a boot boy first appeared in *Marxism Today.* **Joseph Strauss, Germany's right-wing, Tebbo-figure, appeared on the cover of** *Der Spiegel* **equipped with an iron fist.**

Photographs: John Lawrence Jones

Beastly behaviour

Doing people as animals or insects is a technique as old as the art of caricature, which seems to have started as a leisure activity in sixteenth century Italy (though many of the saucier gargoyles on mediaeval cathedrals must be considered part of the tradition). Above: our version of Moshe Dayan, the Israeli war hero, as a desert scorpion was done in 1977 when he was being particularly hard on old political allies. Right: Joseph Luns, the chairman of NATO, was done in the same year as a vulture giving the dove of peace a hard time. Both of these characters were made for *Panorama*, a lively Dutch feature and soft-porn magazine, which gave us regular, if modestly paid, work. Its editor, Jan Heemskerk, would send us a monthly consignment of photographs of people to be caricatured. Very often they would be foreign politicians who we did not know terribly well. If we could not think of anything very subtle to say about them as human beings, we would usually end up turning them into beasts.

Photographs: John Lawrence Jones

the world's top lawyers read
PRIVATE EYE

Point of sale. Luck and Flaw enterprises, like many other labour-intensive industries, operated on very slim profit margins. We therefore tried to supplement our income from newspaper feature work with advertising commissions, though rarely with great success. We like to think that the model, left, made as a point of sale poster for *Private Eye* magazine, was one of the few successes. The characters depicted are Sue, Grabbit and Runn, partners in the mythological firm of libel lawyers dedicated to taking newspapers to the cleaners.

Michael Foot, who succeeded Jim Callaghan as Labour leader after the Party's defeat in the 1979 General Election, was more to our liking than most politicians, yet we were able to show him very little mercy, right. From his flowing locks down to his funny walk he was God's gift to caricaturists, especially as these attributes combined with the air of an olde worlde liberal constantly surprised by the crudities of the modern age. In this study we see him innocently unbandaging a bad foot and encountering the party's beetle-browed, right-wing bruiser, Denis Healey.

Photographs: John Lawrence Jones

Royal occasions

As Luck and Flaw enterprises developed we found ourselves more frequently keeping royal

company. Above: in 1980 Fluck and I were privileged enough to have a pint with the Queen in a Cambridge public house, an event that was recorded for posterity by the BBC *Arena* television programme. The queen in this instance was not one of those gruesome lookalikes, but a genuinely real and concerned human being called Jeanette Charles.

Above right: our model of the Queen and Philip having a cosy cup of tea to celebrate her Jubilee Year figured on the cover of the *Sunday Times* magazine.

Right: the royal couple lunches on a corgi. This image literally girdled the globe. Appearing in Germany's *Stern* magazine and on the cover of the Australian edition of *Time* magazine, it now, with this publication, completes its journey back to Europe.

Left: this study of Prince Charles and Princess Diana with their baby son was actually delivered before Prince William. The baby's ears are therefore works of pure imagination. Called "The Shape of Kings to Come", this image appeared in a book produced by the team of the BBC's comedy programme *Not the Nine 0'Clock News*.

We never actually contributed to this show though we were invited. The producer John Lloyd, who subsequently produced *Spitting Image*, asked us to make a couple of puppets for it, but could not offer us enough money to keep us in supplies of Superglue. He then asked us to weed out enough old transparencies of our models to make a rotating horror item at the end of the show. We singled out 32 and Lloyd said it was not enough to have any impact. "Three years' work," groaned Fluck, "not enough for ten seconds' television."

Photographs: BBC,

John Lawrence Jones

my relief from these adventures in the chapel would be to go down to London one day a week and teach at the Hornsey College of Art. I always liked teaching because there is nearly always something you can pass on, perhaps not so much a skill but something more like a set of connections. All illustration has its family tree, and if you know about the tree you can introduce young people to branches of it that might engage their interest or, better still, enthusiasm. Paul Hogarth did something like this for Fluck and myself and I felt it was something I could do for others. I think I managed it to some extent at Hornsey but perhaps not so well at the Central School, to which I ill-advisedly transferred. The fault was not in the students, but in some of the staff, who seemed to me to be absurdly pretentious.

One day I took all the newspapers, from the *Sun* to the *Guardian*, into the Central and doled them out to my class with the request that they each design a front page with as its main banner headline, "The Queen is Dead." Anyone who has seen a newspaper backbench going into convulsions at the news of the Queen going anywhere near a hospital would realise I was paying these students the compliment of setting them one of the toughest tasks in journalism. And anyone who had not seen such a thing should at least be able to perceive that the task was demanding, but I was hauled in by the department head and

reprimanded for setting the students "a frivolous exercise". The real frivolity, unhappily, was in much of the formal teaching, which was of the how-to-design-a-rain-map-for-Swaziland variety, esoteric and off-putting. I taught there against the prevailing ethos for a while until the moment when I had to leave came to me with extreme clarity. A young student there showed me four sheets of stunning artwork in colour, all just based on household objects, and I said, "These are absolutely beautiful. You really should go to art school."

Within the partnership there was a powerful amount of education going on. One caricature we did for *National Lampoon* featured the Euro-cop, based on the simple notion of a policeman laying into a demonstrator with his truncheon. We did it with a lot of ketchup and it was very, very gory. We also did a sanitised version without any ketchup for a European publication. The fascinating thing was that the sanitised version came out visually much more horrific than the gory one. This, we realised, was because in the cleaned-up version the person looking at the image felt as if they were participating in the brutal act that was just about to happen. The ostensibly more brutal picture, on the other hand, was of something that had already happened in which the viewer had no participation and therefore no emotional involvement.

A more predictable discovery was the difficulty of caricaturing people or characters you positively liked. I doubt whether P.G. Wodehouse could have a greater admirer than me. On my trips to America I would always read him at 30,000 feet to ensure, if anything went wrong, that I would go down laughing. So we were delighted when an American publisher asked us to model

The modelled couples pictured above appeared as a series in *Men Only* entitled "Holiday Romances", though our own working title for it was "nightmare couples". Left to right: Mrs Thatcher nuzzles a deeply alarmed Johnnie Rotten of the Sex Pistols; an elderly Mae West tests her allure on the movie director Roman Polanski, more noted for liking a younger class of person; Ian Smith, the white man's political choice in Southern Rhodesia, paws an anxious Diana Ross; Princess Margaret and Anthony Armstrong-Jones, before they split up.
Photographs: Luck and Flaw

Bertie, Jeeves and Aunt Agatha, but we never got them remotely right.

As the only member of the partnership with a driving licence Fluck was automatically the transport officer, responsible for driving the models down to London where they could be photographed at their best in the studio of our heroic young photographer, John Lawrence Jones. Loading the Citroën Dyane with the models was always a major event. To prevent them smashing each other to pieces on the journey we used to have to cement them to the steel floor of the vehicle with lumps of hot plasticine. I used to brew up the old plasticine and hurl great gobs of it down from the upper level of the chapel onto Fluck as he stood by the car below. And Fluck would leap up and down with rage, not having my keen sense of humour.

The humour of John Lawrence Jones also proved a little shaky when we punched holes in his sets, and generally wrecked his studio in pursuit of the right lighting formulae for *A Christmas Carol*, but he came through it all more heroic than ever. Fluck and I always considered that a good photograph could add forty per cent to the quality of the models, which was why we considered it was worth taking them to a specialist studio in London rather than getting a photographer to come to the chapel to take snaps. If our models were in any way more vivid than those of Daumier and other model-makers in the past, it was almost entirely due to developments in colour photography. We were lucky in the technology of our age, much as Aubrey Beardsley, whose black ink style coincided so perfectly with the development of the line block, was lucky in his. Arguably, Charles Keene was Beardsley's superior as a draughtsman but we only got to see his work in the cruder form of wood engravings.

By the end of the seventies Luck and Flaw was a truly international business. Our study of Jimmy Carter had gone right round the world and even Venezuela had coughed up its £30 royalty fee. Our presentation of the Queen and Prince Philip feasting on corgi appeared not only in *Stern* magazine, which commissioned the work, but also on the cover of the Australian edition of *Time* magazine. In Britain we still serviced *The Economist* and the *Radio Times* and occasionally the *Sunday Times*, where we had become a mild flavour again, not I think because we were much admired, but because they didn't want to be left out. The *Sunday Times* business, in any event, tended to be on the ultra cautious side. We did an excellent study of the comedian Bernard Manning throttling a microphone in the shape of a Pakistani for the *Sunday Times*, but it never appeared. If we wanted to do anything at all racy, like the new Tory Cabinet in full frontal nude, we would have to turn to outlets like *Men Only*.

Along with the international reputation, we were also enjoying a little of the notoriety that our personalities so pathetically craved. Anglia television and the BBC's *Arena* outfit both did programmes about us. Anthony Wall, the producer of the *Arena* programme who became a friend, billed us handsomely as the most famous unknown illustrators in Britain.

Our first acquaintance with Jimmy Carter was two grubby photographs in the *New York Times'* library labelled "John Carter". His being so little known gave wings to our caricature when he achieved prominence. Left: the model for the *New York Times*. Above: how it appeared in *Stern* and the *Sunday Times*.

Photograph: Bob Cramp

Previous pages: Jimmy Carter as a "lame duck" President in the summer of 1980, covered in wounds inflicted by cares of state and by falls sustained while jogging. This model looked nothing like Carter on leaving the bench, but was redeemed by the subtlety of John Lawrence Jones' lighting.

We made our first fully upholstered body for the model of the comedian Bernard Manning, seen here throttling a microphone in the shape of a Pakistani. It was ordered by the *Sunday Times* but was not used, despite all the ingenuity and raw material that had gone into its construction.

Photographs: John Lawrence Jones

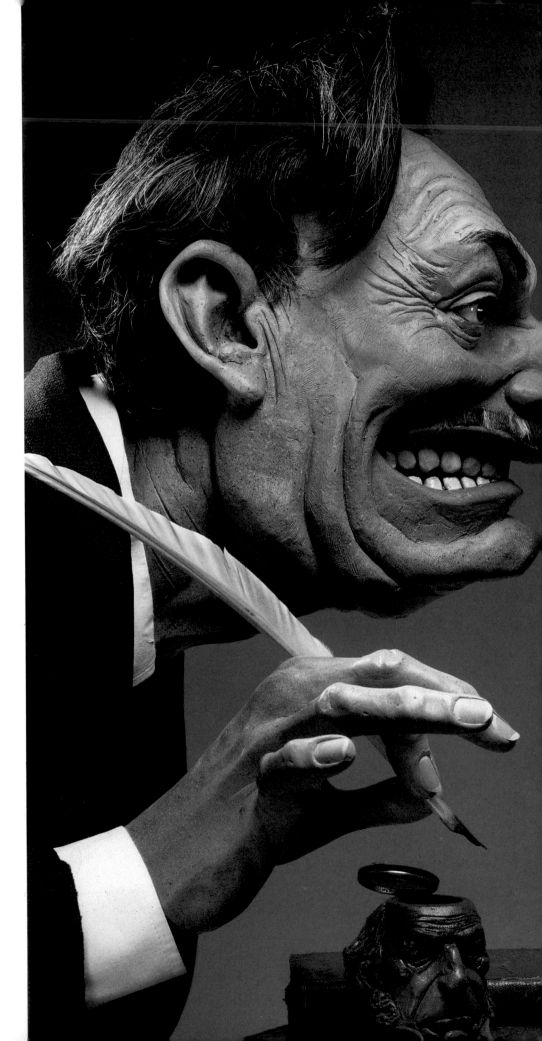

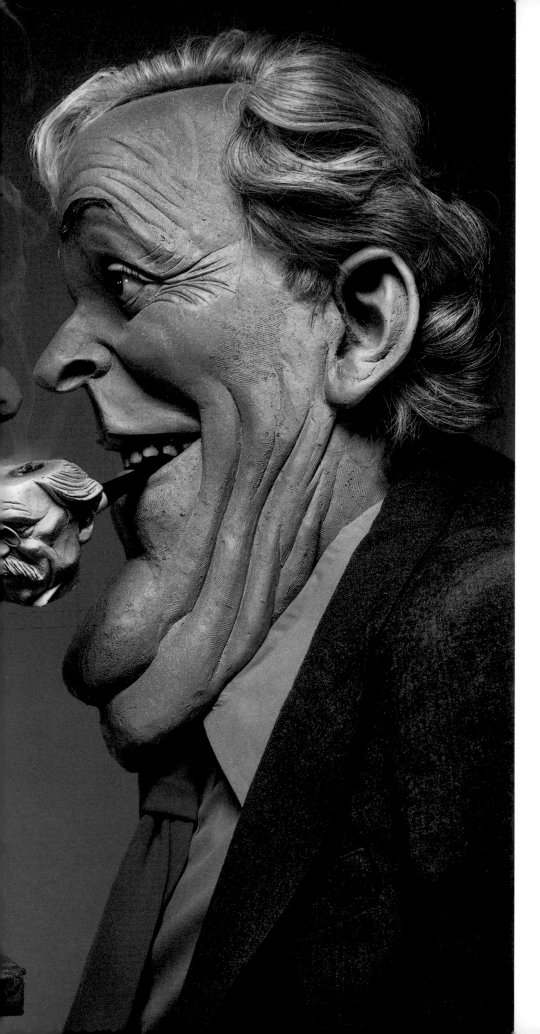

A unique moment of intimacy between Enoch Powell and Tony Benn is captured in this model for the *Sunday Times* in February 1983. The occassion for it was a TV series called *Number Ten* dealing with the exploits of former Prime Ministers - see Benn's pipe for Ramsay MacDonald, Powell's inkwell for Gladstone - which Powell and Benn discussed for the magazine. By this time we felt our model caricature had reached quite a high standard, but this was about as far as it would go. By the end of the year we were engulfed by the cruder demands of *Spitting Image*.

Photograph: John Lawrence Jones

Champagne fascists

We had a request for three carnival heads for an Anti-Nazi League rally in Victoria Park. We did them an expenses-only Hitler and two home-grown fascists, John Tyndall and Martin Webster. This page: the various stages of Webster's construction. Fluck used champagne glasses to shape

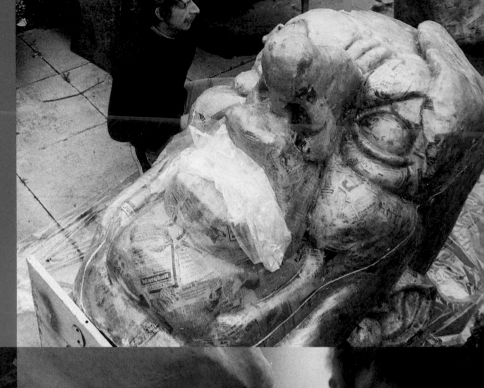

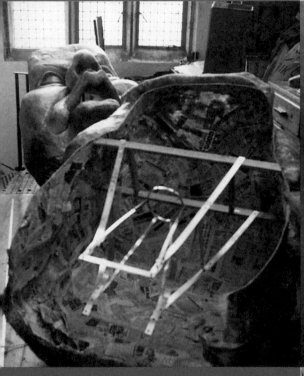

their eyes. Far right: how Webster appeared at the rally. The main raw material used in his construction was cheap polyurethane foam. The rally organiser asked if, as a climax, they could burn the heads. We advised against it, unless he wanted to asphyxiate the crowd.

Main photograph: David King

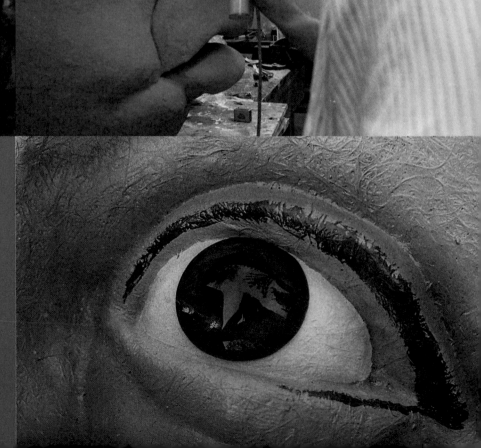

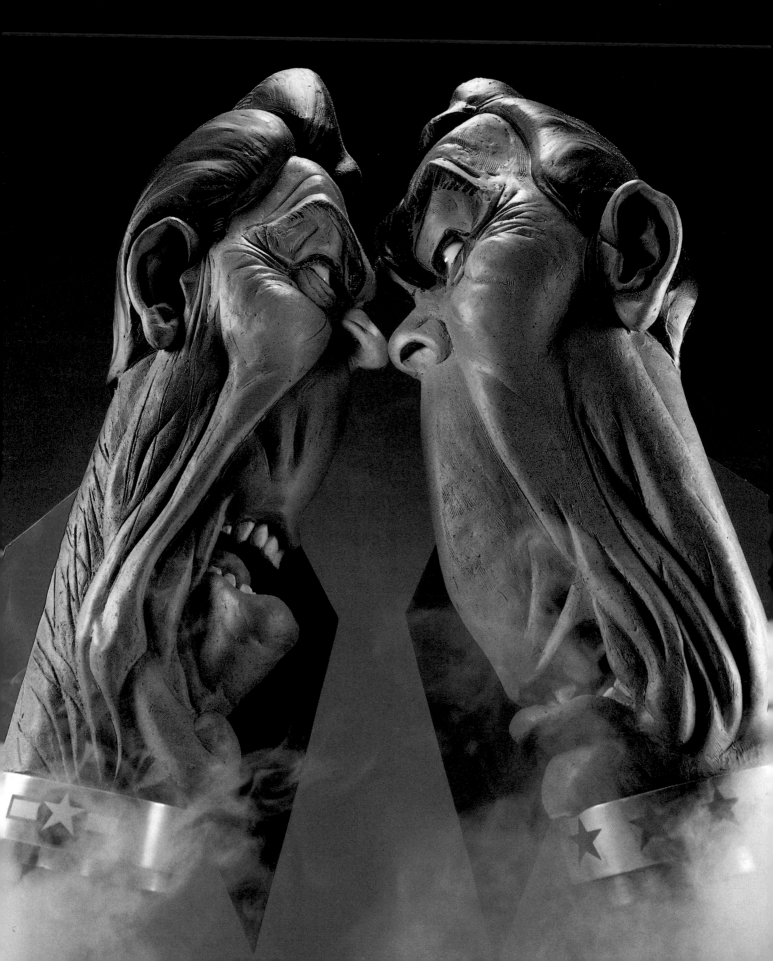

We were also going broke. The problem with the global business was that while it was wide, it was quite exceptionally thin. All the overseas stuff was done on perilously fragile margins, and the British market was not that hot either. For filling a space in a magazine or newspaper, which was essentially what we did, we might be paid a little over the rate for the page, but not much. A cartoonist or a photographer working on their own might be able to fill that space with a day's work, whereas no matter how hard I lashed Fluck, or how much he needled me, the two of us could never produce a decent model, properly photographed, in much less than a week.

It was a hard thing to realise that cornering the international market in grotesques was about as economically rewarding as being a gardener in an Oxbridge college. On the other hand, I don't think that either of us regretted the decision to go it alone together, so to speak, on our home turf. Fluck's idea of heaven was to trick himself out in waders and give any trout in the vicinity a miserable time and this activity was more accessible in Cambridge than it had been in Kensington. For my part, I very much appreciated the advantages of working so close to home so that I could watch Shem, Sophie and Sophie's rabbits growing up. Unlike the children, the rabbits were showing encouraging signs of not wanting to go to art school.

Freed from chores on the models, Deirdre was able to pursue her interest in patchwork and quilting, where her use of complex "colour wash" techniques would earn her an international reputation as both designer and teacher. Among the overseas places that sought her advice was Soweto in South Africa, and she visited the township on a couple of occasions. I can remember a return match when the ladies of Soweto came to visit us in Orchard Street. It's well known that Soweto is the worst slum in Africa. Less well known is the fact that it has an awesome, house-proud bourgeoisie, and I could tell from the horrified expressions of the contingent of black ladies in our dishevelled living room that our housekeeping was way below their accustomed standards.

Despite the highly connubial nature of our existences, there was no concealing the fact that the most important woman in the lives of Fluck and myself was becoming Mrs Margaret Thatcher. Very soon after her election in 1979 I remember telling Hugo Young, then the deeply sagacious political correspondent on the *Sunday Times*, what a laugh her manifesto was, full of ridiculous pledges that never would be kept. Young felt he should advise me not to get too carried away with mirth, because she definitely was not joking. We did her for the *Sunday Times* as an Iron Maiden covered in heavy metal kitchen utensils.

Hotting up the Cold War. The election of Ronald Reagan as President of the United States in 1980 seemed to place an itchier trigger finger on the nuclear button. To illustrate CND's reawakened apprehensions we did Reagan and the Russian leader, Leonid Brezhnev, as nuclear missiles for the peace movement publication, *Sanity*, left. For the *Sunday Times*, above, we did the folksy Reagan, with his scene-stealing wife Nancy, inhabiting the American Dream and having an apple-blossom time.

Photographs: John Lawrence Jones

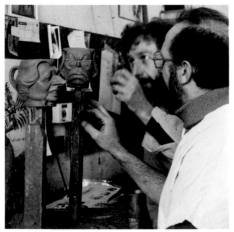

Above: our Mrs Thatcher teapot. Far left: Fluck consults with Graham Loughton, our master moulder advisor. Near left: a *Private Eye* **advertisement for our royal output. Right: Fluck and I pose as old artisans for a brochure picture designed to boost our business. From the sales figures, it appears that nobody was fooled.**

Photographs: Above, John Lawrence Jones. Right, Peter Moody Meyer

STOCK
SHELVES
INVESTMENTS

THE YEAR
SCROOGE
THEORY...

We were drawn to Charles Dickens' book *A Christmas Carol* because his work seemed to lend itself to our style of illustration, and for another more specific reason. Dickens never wrote a shorter book. Even so, it took us well over a year to produce all the models, miniaturise all their little props and sets, and get them photographed in living colour. Above: a working drawing for Bob Cratchit. Right: Cratchit in the counting house.
Photograph: John Lawrence Jones

Less successfully, Fluck and I tried to do her as a hen for the *Arena* programme. Through our agricultural connections we found a brilliant hen, which could do practically anything. We kitted her out with a Mrs Thatcher mask and rehearsed her carefully to defecate over some "Top Secret" Cabinet papers on a desk. But when the cameras were on she only seemed to be interested in undoing the cameraman's shoelaces. In the end I just took her home with me, where she defecated over everything.

We also made, for popular usage, several thousand Mrs Thatcher teapots which, aside from certain deficiencies, like a tendency to break the wrist of anyone over thirty and to scald hands of all ages, were really very fine objects. Unfortunately, outside Northern Ireland, where they appeared to think it was a Tory central office promotion, it did not sell in significant numbers. We therefore had plenty to spare when Anglia TV came round to make their little programme. The final question they asked was, "And why should anyone buy a Mrs Thatcher teapot?" With uncanny foresight we had managed to anticipate this question and had set up three Mrs Thatcher teapots on a glass table. As the camera panned over them I moved in with a large hammer and smashed the lot. At this point the commentator's voice, unscripted by us, said, "What a wonderful way to earn a living."

Somehow we attracted the attention of a character called Robert Putz, who was an exceptionally enjoyable German businessman. He came into the chapel one day and ingratiated himself by saying, "Chennelmen, I am going to make you both millionaires." Putz saw us making a unique and lucrative contribution to the advertising industry. As part of this contribution he had us making, theoretically for Nikon Cameras, a rainbow with a puzzled chameleon in front of it. One day we were humping this enormous chameleon around when it hit us simultaneously that never in eight million years was this idea going work. So the chorus went up, "What a wonderful way to earn a living."

It was becoming clear that our vigorous efforts to sell out on the advertising and merchandising fronts were both going no place fast. An accountant we called in to advise us on ceramic sales said that we would be in a more profitable line if we went out on the street and bought pound notes for £1.50 a time.

We could have laughed this off but for the fact that our traditional market was also shrinking. We managed to get *A Christmas Carol* out, but *Treasure Island*, on which we felt we had done a terrific job, was stalled, endlessly waiting for a publisher ready to take on the expense of its production. More worryingly, it was becoming apparent that the general feature magazines, always our staple outlet, were all headed down the same dread consumerist road that led to *Lifestyles* and *Living Kitchens* and the most attenuated human horizons.

Luck and Flaw enterprises was, in short, on the verge of discovering a wonderful way not to earn a living when a man announcing himself as Martin Lambie-Nairn came on the telephone and invited us out to lunch.

Working drawings for the character of Scrooge, attempting to distil the essence of "a squeezing, wrenching, grasping, scraping, clutching, covetous old sinner". Above: how Scrooge appeared on the cover of our book. Far right: Scrooge with a Jacob Marley rendered ghostly by tricks of double exposure with John Lawrence Jones' camera. Overleaf: Mr Fezziwig's Ball. The creation of a diarama with 26 models on armatures dancing, smooching and making merry was among Peter Fluck's finest achievements.

Photographs: John Lawrence Jones

150

Publand pirates

For Robert Louis Stevenson's classic tale, *Treasure Island*, we went life-size with the modelling. We based the characters on mates we drank with in Cambridge pubs, some of whom were more frightening than the pirates in the story (see Kevin far right). We had great times making *Treasure Island* even though the life-size "Long John" Silver almost killed me by wrestling me over the chapel bannisters. The book was planned as a sequel to *A Christmas Carol* but the expense of its production kept it on the stocks for years. It was eventually published in 1986, after *Spitting Image* had added a little lustre to our notoriety. Above: Fluck blows smoke for misty dawn effect in the "Flag of Truce" episode. Right: Fluck and I enact: "the deadly wrestle" between Hands and his companion. Above right: "the deadly wrestle" in the book illustration. Overleaf: the pirates storm the stockade, led by Kevin's lookalike. Following pages left: Captain Billy Bones. Right: John Silver.

Main photographs:

John Lawrence Jones

Martin Lambie-Nairn was an attractive, gnome-like man who did the graphics for current affairs

shows at London Weekend Television. In the course of his work he was much struck by the discrepancy between what was said by the nation's leading politicians on camera, and what they said in the privacy of the hospitality room after the show. Being of a thoughtful, if somewhat unconventional nature - at LWT he was best known for his habit of playing bagpipes on the roof and for a then wholly unfashionable addiction to born-again Christianity - Lambie-Nairn pondered long and hard on how this intriguing phenomenon could be translated into some form of television. One night, in the winter of 1981, he had a secular vision of a show employing a new, grown-up generation of Muppets. Hence our invitation to lunch.

First, Smash Your Parrot

Photograph: David King

Martin Lambie-Nairn, the graphic designer at London Weekend Television, who bought a lunch for Peter Fluck and myself which took us over two years to digest.

Of the many nice things about Lambie-Nairn, the nicest, from the point of view of Fluck and myself, was that he had some money. The idea in itself was not that novel. Fluck and I had been talking and fantasising about making the models move, almost since the partnership began. One of the main parties to these fruitless conversations was Pat Gavin, once a student of mine at Hornsey School of Art who had risen, via experience in animation films, to the dizzying height of head of graphics at LWT. It was Gavin who pointed Lambie-Nairn in our direction, and it was Gavin who alerted us to the need to refrain from eating our peas from off our knives during the lunch.

We were rewarded with Lambie-Nairn's proposal, which was that his graphics firm, which was doing quite well, should invest some of its surplus cash in a Muppet-style political television programme. It looked as if the cash could be enough to fund our efforts for as long as six months. Would we be interested? Despite my lingering aversion to puppets, we had no hesitation in saying that we would be delighted to spend his firm's money. It would be another two years, by which time we would spend several other people's money, including what was left of our own, before we had anything worthwhile to show for this initiative.

There are three basic approaches to animation, and we had looked at them all over the years. The classic approach, made famous by Walt Disney, is cell animation, in which movement in the characters is produced by hundreds upon hundreds of drawings, tracing their activity frame by frame, not unlike a flick book. But what was good enough for *Sleeping Beauty* and *Pinocchio* and for Chuck Jones' *Bugs Bunny* did not seem appropriate. There was another consideration. Full cell animation could come in at up to £1,000 a second which, on the basis of the original budget, would have us into overspend after ten seconds' worth of animation.

A more accessible form of animation is stop motion, most brilliantly deployed in recent times in the electricity industry advertisements fashioned by the Oscar-winning Nick Park of Aardman in Bristol. In this type of animation you started out with three-dimensional figures, not vastly different from the ones we were already making, and then moved them by very slow degrees, clicking away at each halt to build up the animation, again frame by frame. We were initially very attracted to stop motion, but the constraint we kept coming up against was time. It had always been part of our notion that the models should move in a topical environment. There was no way, that Pat Gavin could see, that stop motion could be fast enough.

We came then, almost by default, to the third main form of animation, namely puppetry, in which the animation is provided by concealed human limbs usually, though not invariably, arms and hands. The advantage of puppets is that they can be filmed in real time but I was not, from my own experience of filming them at Reed College, capable of being persuaded that puppets on strings was a realistic way ahead. There were, however, in Jim Henson's Muppets, graphic examples of what could be achieved by puppeteers using direct hands-up-the-throat techniques.

Despite the huge success of the Muppets we were by no means convinced that this approach was entirely right for us. I remember going to a lecture by Henson in which he explained that the Muppets were successful precisely because they were not people. With Kermit - a piece of green rag with two ping pong balls for eyes - there were no problems of credibility, he was a veritable frog. Henson thought it unlikely that anyone could achieve the same necessary suspension of disbelief with puppet people.

We thought it might be possible, but only with the most sophisticated puppetry that could be found, and that, we reasoned, meant getting seriously acquainted with the film industry. It was clear from films like *Star Wars* and *Greystoke* that the movies were light years ahead of other media in terms of special effects. Our original idea was that we should design the puppets while the film people, with their advanced notions of radio-control and how to make noses explode, would kit them out. This was a wrong turning right from the very start, which set us back at least eighteen months.

By the autumn of 1982 our star caricature, Nancy the Parrot, designed to perch on President Reagan's pirate shoulder, had enough metal in her head to fly to the moon. Mechanised controls governed the head, neck and eyelid movements, while the beak, tongue and wings were hand-operated. She was coming in at around £6,000 and for our purposes she was worse than useless. With any luck she would blink on command on one occasion out of five.

What we had totally failed to grasp was the fact film puppets are essentially one performance creatures. If they could blink or roar or pick their noses once in close-up, it was quite enough. But we needed puppets that could credibly go a distance, or at least the length of a pilot programme. The effect of Nancy the Parrot on the morale of our backers, who now included the Cambridge inventor-businessman Clive Sinclair, can readily be imagined. They would send emissaries round to the chapel to monitor progress but, aside from Nancy's increases in weight to accommodate new non-functioning mechanisms, there was none. Fluck, who emerged as the diplomat of the partnership at this stage, would tell them that we were making great strides in learning what not to do.

What we had to do quite simply was start all over. This was precisely what we did but not soon enough to retain Sinclair's sponsorship. He pulled out after investing £20,000 in the venture. Fortunately, John Banks, the Cambridge

The Gang of Five who launched
Spitting Image **consisted of Peter Fluck and myself; John Lloyd, top; Tony Hendra, seen snarling below Lloyd, and Jon Blair, seen putting our stars at ease.**

Birth pangs of *Spitting Image* in the chapel. Fluck demonstrates an early puppet eye movement; Steve Bendelack, our first employee, cradles a newborn prototype puppet, while I pause from a long and searching study of earlier form in the constant quest for inspiration.
Photograph: Phil Sayer

Above left: we made Prince Charles and Prince Philip as glove puppets for an early version of the *Spitting Image* pilot programme. But we soon decided to abandon them in favour of larger, arm-up-the-throat models. Almost ten years later glove puppets made a comeback. We now use them in the *Spitting Image* title sequence, where their readily adaptable nature makes late changes possible.

Above right: some characters we made for the pilot programme. Among the most notable were the androgynous figure on the right, doubling as Queen Victoria and Alfred Hitchcock, and the head in the centre representing Menachem Begin, Israel's Prime Minister. Begin starred in a conjuror's hat from which he produced a dove which he promptly strangled.

Photograph: Peter Moody Meyer

business consultant who was our contact with Sinclair, was able to limit some of the financial damage by recruiting another backer. But the main skill I developed in this period was a trust-me, Arthur Daley telephone manner when assuring our suppliers that their cheques were in the post.

Things only really started to look up when we smashed Nancy, and Fluck distributed her bits and pieces into three other puppets. As it turned out, we were quite capable of making small conventional latex puppets ourselves. Eye movements were a problem but Fluck was confident he could crack it. The biggest problem for both of us was trying to eradicate some of the responses we had spent twenty years learning in newspapers and magazines.

With a newspaper caricature you would invariably start off with the idea, or the joke, before you even thought of reaching for the plasticine, because this would determine whether you wanted your character to be full face or profile and what its expression should be. When it came to puppet-creation, however, the one-joke approach was of no value. We had to go against our natural grain and find more neutral expressions that would make our characters capable of telling a lot of jokes, most of them not of our devising.

By late 1982 our three main jokers were assembled with us in a company called Spitting Image. This formed a puppet control group, popularly known as the Gang of Five. The first to join us was Tony Hendra, our old mate from the *National Lampoon*, whom we judged to be the funniest. Hendra was the man who invented the "Not" concept, producing publications like *Not the Bible* and *Not the New York Times*. The second to arrive was John Lloyd, a young but experienced broadcaster who had borrowed the "Not" concept to produce *Not the Nine O'Clock News*, a successful BBC comedy programme starring Rowan Atkinson. The third to arrive was Jon Blair, a documentary producer, who was not really funny at all, just incredibly effective.

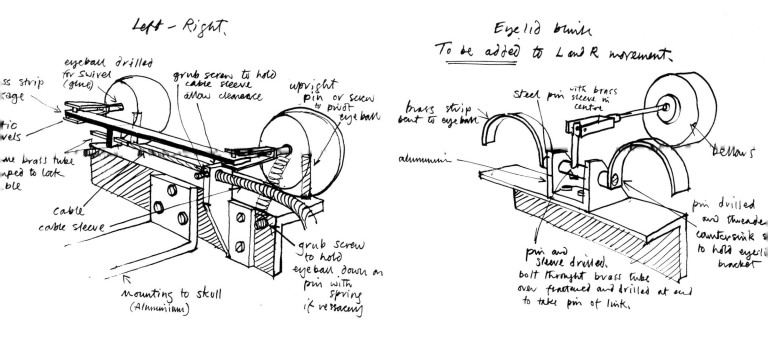

It was Blair who lifted us all out of the quagmire created by Sinclair's departure. He hawked our flimsy wares round the television network and ultimately managed to couple us with Central Television, which agreed to underwrite our further endeavours. Thus the last lap of the research process - making a pilot programme - was done in some style.

Produced by John Lloyd and directed by Philip Casson, a former *Muppets* director, the *Spitting Image* pilot programme was shot at Ewart Studios in Wandsworth in June 1983, and it turned out rather well. The sketch which lives on in the memory was the one about the five Japanese samurai trying to impress their Emperor with ever more bizarre methods of committing hari kiri. My favourite was the one who sliced off the top of his head with a sword and then reached for a grapefruit knife to work round the rim of his severed skull. He then added a glacé cherry and a sliver of orange on a cocktail stick to the skull's contents before eating them with what remained of his head. This proved fatal to the samurai and very nearly extinguished his puppeteer.

More important than our liking it was the fact that Charles Denton, Central's director of programmes, was ecstatic about it.

There was a golden glow over the party to celebrate the success of the pilot. Held in the water meadow beside Fluck's elegant residence in Duxford, a few miles from Cambridge, it was a gathering of all those who had made it possible, including the freshly knighted Sir Clive Sinclair, whose good spirits were in no way impaired by the unexpected prospect of getting his money back. The sun shone down throughout a proceeding already well toasted by the warmth of mutual admiration. But what made the party was the fact that Fluck's two young children, Penny and Robert, and all their neighbourhood mates, never came out into the garden. They just sat indoors with their mouths agape, watching the pilot video, over and over again.

One of the toughest puppet problems we had to solve was credible eye movement. The mechanisms on offer to us from the film industry cost £800 a piece and were less than wholly reliable. Fluck cracked the problem with a cheap brass and cable arrangement, but the secrets of its manufacture remained in his head. One day Fluck went into hospital to have treatment for a sceptic shoulder, leaving *Spitting Image* virtually eyeless. Under torture, and the influence of morphine, he produced the diagrams, above.

Nightmare in Dockland

Chapter 10 The World's First Ever Caricature Factory was established in what had once been a rum and banana warehouse. Located in the ghostly West India Docks, amid a dark forest of giant, motionless cranes, it looked like the kind of place where great enterprises came to lie down and die. For all that, it had hidden charms, the principal one being that you could get a lot of space there for not a lot of rent.

Photographs: David King

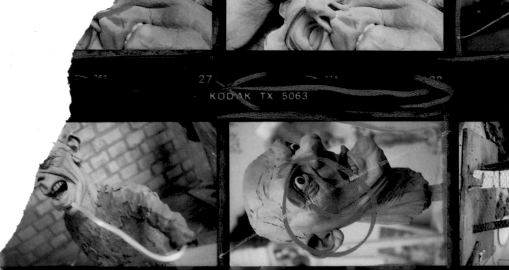

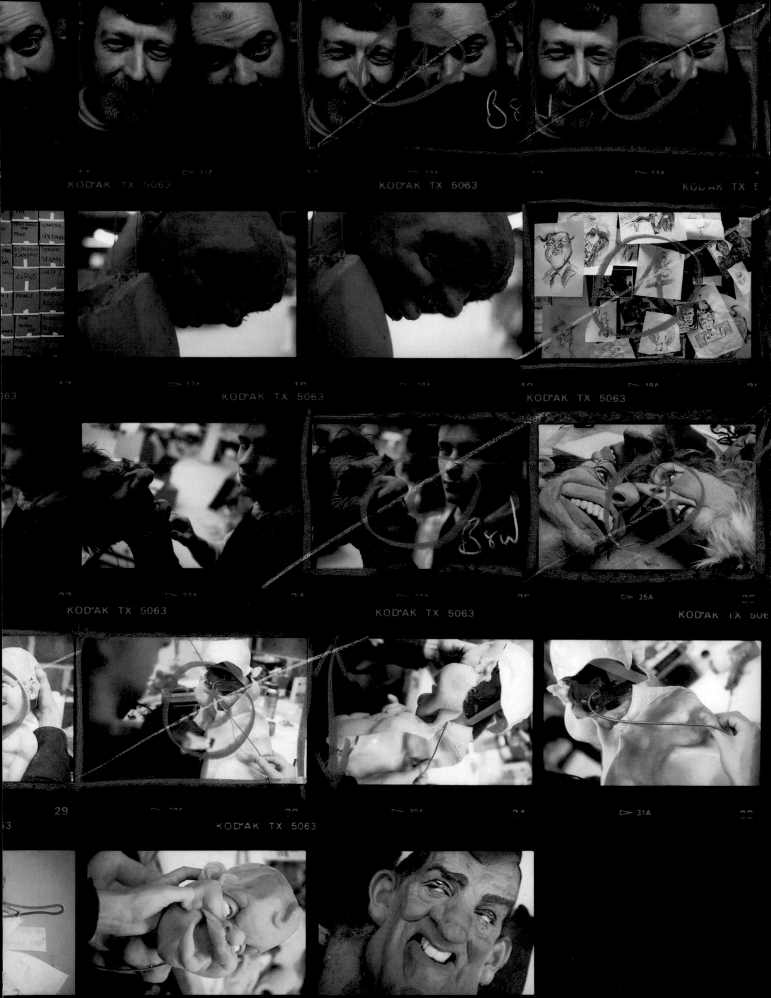

We were sorry to leave the chapel but it had hardly been big enough to cope with the R and D for *Spitting Image* . The move from the chapel to East London was accomplished in a pantechnicon loaned to us by Central Television. On arrival, Fluck and I discovered that our twenty-five models, prototypes for the first puppets, each had a stick pointing out of the top of their heads. They had been impaled with their own armatures. We knew exactly how they must feel.

In truth, though, when set beside the early days of *Spitting Image*, a hole in the head would have made a most refreshing experience. I remember those days as the worst period in my life. Fluck has a similar recollection.

To be on the job at all hours we set up a working home in Star Lane, Canning Town, in a small house owned by Hendra's sister, on the edge of a perfectly preserved bomb site. Hendra, Fluck and I lived there with our first workshop employee, Steve Bendelack, in what proved to be the most torrid circumstances. Our evenings would be spent drinking together and infecting one another with pessimistic news from different parts of the battlefield. There was absolutely nothing to relieve the tension and tension is among the worst enemies of a sense of humour. There was a funny side to the ménage but all we could see was the oppression of what we had got ourselves into. We were quite literally terrified of our own show, with some good reason.

We had taken five months preparing for the pilot, grooming it lovingly all the while. Now we were confronted with having to make thirteen shows for delivery in successive weeks. This entailed a production schedule which laid down that, at any one time, three shows would be going through different phases of preparation. And just to simplify matters, Central had insisted that the shows be shot at their Birmingham studios. So our magnificent creations would be forever jolting up and down the M1, either *en route* to stardom or coming back for badly needed repairs.

The enormity of it all was compounded by a knock-down-and-drag-out, deeply unfunny struggle between our funniest men, which had a poisonous effect on the vibes in Star Lane. Jon Blair had wisely opted for administrative duties in Birmingham, but Lloyd, the show's producer, and Hendra, the scripts supremo, were locked in what looked like an irresolvable conflict about what the puppets should say. Hendra was more inclined to have outrageous characters, like all Russians as bears for example, and for deploying them in regular sit-coms. Lloyd was more in favour of lookalike characters, which he felt would give the show more flexibility, and he saw them as operating most effectively in shorter, sharper sketches.

The war between the conceptions ran right through the planning stages

and halfway through the first series until Hendra, ultimately defeated, returned to the United States. It was a relief to have the struggle over and done, but there was no rejoicing. In the final days, I had been for Lloyd, while Fluck had been for Hendra. It was, by a long way, the most painful disagreement we had ever had. The only pleasing consequence of it all was the end of the Star Lane co-habitation policy, out of which Fluck fashioned one of his rules of existence: "Those who are not getting on during the day, should not drink together in the evenings."

The first sight of our models moving on national television was a cringe-making experience. We were already under par because of a row with Central which had eliminated the star of our show. Peter Harris, the *Muppets*-turned-*Spitting Image* director was confident that the Queen would emerge triumphantly as "our Miss Piggy". But the board of Central had ruled that she should not appear so as not to embarrass Prince Philip, who was opening the company's Nottingham studio the following week. The even greater surprise for Fluck and myself was how awful the puppets looked.

The crude television glare seemed to maximise their every defect. It was as if the hours we had spent with John Lawrence Jones getting our models lit to best effect, had gone for nothing. It being television, we were more likely to be judged on how these creatures looked and, to our eyes, they looked bad. This

A still of John and Norma Major eating peas. In the early days we believed the jokes had to come fast and furious to disguise the inept acting of the puppets. Latterly, we have been able to throttle down as their acting has improved beyond recognition - the performance of the puppet Prime Minister is the best evidence of this development.

The Docklands caricature
factory. While the gaffers confer,
the workers nervously huddle.
Photograph: David King

aggravation would lead to one of the more famous exchanges on the studio floor, when Fluck, totally usurping the lighting director's authority, commanded, "Turn out half the lights." "Which half?" came the subtle reply but Fluck, not about to be blinded by science, roared back: "Any half."

The problem in Birmingham, as Fluck so elegantly put it, was that we did not know what we were doing and they did not know what had hit them. When *Spitting Image* was being made the studio floor, accustomed for twenty years to the stately measures of *Crossroads*, would look like a cross between a madhouse and a slaughterhouse. There would be heads and bits of bodies all over the shop and puppeteers on the verge of dementia trying to synchronise awkward latex mouths with pre-recorded in-character voices. There would be amazing creatures with six legs preening themselves in front of mirrors which, on close inspection, would be revealed as an effort at co-ordination between three puppeteers, one operating the head and arm, one operating the other arm, and one working the eye movement.

While all this incredibly chaotic and un-*Crossroads*-like activity was going on and causing upset in the studio, the men in suits could not help noticing that we were breaking all the wrong kind of records. It was the most expensive comedy show on television (the first series cost well over £2 million) and, by a million miles, the slowest to produce. It would take one hour of studio time, television's most sacred commodity, to produce one screenable minute of *Spitting Image*.

In television terms there had never been a beast quite like it. One of the paradoxes of *Spitting Image* was that while it was a wholly original show, it contained virtually nothing that was new. Practically all the elements were as old as either Punch or Judy or John Logie Baird's invention of "seeing with wireless". The historical first was assembling a cast of puppeteers, costumiers, voice-impressionists, mould-makers, TV cameramen, foam experts, set-builders, funny writers, model-makers from the Fens and electricians recently made redundant by the motor industry, and expecting them to work harmoniously together, without any previous experience of so doing. Eventually, some degree of harmony would be achieved, but there would be precious little in the first series. John Lloyd would describe the task of producing the whole works as "like pulling a dinosaur backwards by its tail".

This gathering of expert skills made it very difficult for anyone who worked in the show to actually see it. All people could see was how their own specialism had been violated. Thus puppeteers would rage about camera angles allowing their elbows to appear in shot, writers would turn nasty about the mutilation of their punch lines, while the model-makers would winge endlessly on about the lighting. For an objective view of what the show was actually like we were pathetically reliant on the press and the majority of the national newspapers thought it was nowhere near being up to scratch. My old newspa-

pers were among the leading pessimists. The *Observer* thought our initial effort was "a dog", while the *Sunday Times* described it as "slow" and in need of a radical shake-up.

Since Fluck and I had spent almost our entire working lives trying to beguile editors in what is termed the quality press, this was something of a shock to the system. It was even more of a shock to find ourselves eagerly scouring the columns of the *Sun* and the *Star,* where some of the earliest crumbs of comfort to *Spitting Image* were to be found.

It would have been nice to be in a position to blame the censor but there were no serious difficulties after the loss of the Queen in the very first show. Aside from very small disappointments, like the IBA banning a Bernard Levin sketch in which he explained why he became a writer - "I think it was because I was circumcised with a pencil sharpener" - most of what we considered our more outrageous material got in the show. But it just didn't seem to be working.

On parade: puppet heads manufactured in the Limehouse workshop lined up in readiness for transport to the Birmingham studios in their allocated boxes. They travelled in pairs, alphabetically. Thus the Pope spent a lot of time close to Princess Anne, and Ken Livingstone shared a box with Lord Lucan. But sentimental exceptions were made - Torville was boxed with Dean, and Jimmy Greaves with Ian St John.
Photograph: David King

Father knew best

Above: Tim Watts, at seventeen, was the youngest of the child labourers in the *Spitting Image* factory. He originally joined us to help make the models for the pilot programme. His father had first brought him to our attention by writing to say that we should employ his son as he was a genius. As he was about the fiftieth father who had written to us in a similar fashion, we did not take an excessive amount of notice. But we did agree to see Tim and his work, and this particular father turned out to be right.

His only previous experience had been as a schoolboy cartoonist on the *Leicester Mercury*, but it was apparent that he was an instinctive caricaturist. This can be seen, right and above, from his drawing and model of Michael Parkinson, and from working drawings, far right, for Robert Maxwell, Keith Richards, Ringo Starr, Pete Townshend and a brace of Scargills. Among his many notable contributions to the show were the all-nose Manilow and Madonna's singing belly-button. Sadly, Watts got away. He made his escape by going to the Kingston School of Art and now works with the film animator, Dick Williams.

178

VARIOUS INSECTS DESCEND TO ANNOY PROKOVIEV AT BOTTOM OF TREE

PROKOVIEV GRABS PETER OFF TO COTTAGE SEQUENCE 7.

BIRD & DUCK SHOW DISAPPROVAL.

INSIDE THE COTTAGE PETER & PROKOVIEV ARGUE OF THE SCORE

PROKOVIEV CROSSES OUT THE WORD ANIMALS AND SUBSTITUTES TO PETERS DELIGHT

ANOTHER WOLF SEQUENCE.

BECOMES   MAJOR   WOLF

ENTRANCE. — GRADUALLY EMERGING DETAILS,

HE COMES OUT ONTO STAGE AMID DRY ICE.

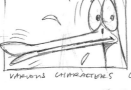

VARIOUS CHARACTERS QUAKE IN CLOSE UP.

HE STALKS THE CAT

WHO JUMPS ON A STAGE LIFT AND ASCENDS THE TREE.

DUCK STAGGERS OUT OF POND & THREATENS WOLF WITH SCOTCH BOTTLE.

SHOT OF DUCK FROM INSIDE WOLFS MOUTH

JAWS SNAP SHUT. TO BLACK.

DUCK INSIDE WOLFS STOMACH. FULL OF SKELETONS ETC DUCK IS NOW SOBER

Head caricaturist

David Stoten, above, seen here hard at work by a pair of royal slippers, joined us when he was twenty-one, after completing his studies at St Martin's School of Art. His previous work experience was as holiday relief on *Mad* magazine. On *Spitting Image* he would rise to the dizzying height of head caricaturist, as Fluck and I moved from the bench into other areas. Above left: His qualifications for the post can be seen in the caricatures of a doglike Alastair Burnet, which doubles as a Burnet-like dog, Ronnie Corbett and *Private Eye's* Ian Hislop. He now does caricatures for Tina Brown's *New Yorker*. Opposite below: meat and two veg. Terry Wogan, as meat, and Sue Lawley, as two veg, were Stoten creations for an *Arena* programme about food. Stoten would eventually cede the title of head caricaturist to · Pablo Bach in order to concentrate on the Spitting Image company's developing interest in stop-motion animation and other diversifications. Opposite above: part of Stoten's storyboard for Prokofiev's *Peter and the Wolf*, which Spitting Image plans to produce in collaboration with the conductor Claudio Abbado.

How to make a puppet

1 In the writers' room it's agreed that the cares of office had sadly aged the Queen. Her puppet will have to be remade.

2 The recent photographic reference arrives and Pablo Bach, the head caricaturist, sketches the new Queen in full-face, profile and various other attitudes.

3 Putting the clay on the stick (armature). Pablo first roughs out a shape for the Queen's head, a key stage in any caricature.

nlike the script and production side of the enterprise, the workshop did not suffer from a divided command. From the outset it was agreed that I should run the workshop while Fluck would ingratiate himself with the natives and whisper warnings in my ear if they seemed to be getting restless. They rarely seemed to be getting anything else. We started out with a workshop staff of eleven, sufficient we thought to cater for all the puppet-making processes - research (of what the characters looked like in real life), drawing, modelling, moulding, foaming (an increasingly essential stage as we moved from little latex characters to big fleshy foam ones), fitting (of eyes and special features, like revolving toupées) and costume. We reckoned to get an individual puppet through all these processes in a week.

Costume was run by Sue Gibson, who had been at art school with us, but in all other areas we employed child labour, partly for exploitative reasons and partly because we sensed that the workshop would be no place for people old enough to be already aware of having a breaking-point. This was shrewd thinking but when Lloyd won the final script battle with Hendra, it proved nothing like shrewd enough. The new short, sharp sketch regime immediately

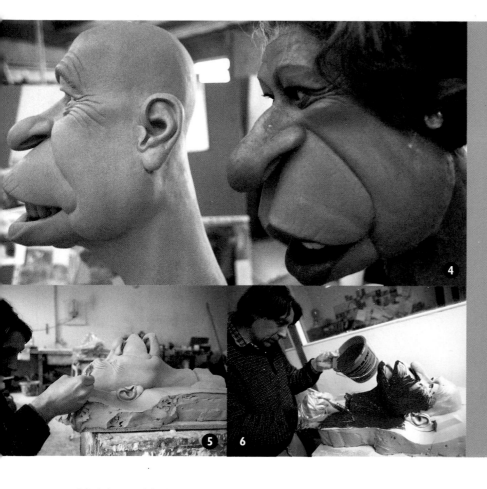

4 The finished clay model, hairless but detailed in every other respect.

5 Steve Haines, the mould-maker, lays up the head on a clay bed, in preparation for the fibre glass mould.

6 Applying the red fibreglass to one half. He then applies it to the other half.

trebled the weekly demand for new puppets. There was no alternative, we just had to conscript more children.

The two we worked with most closely were Tim Watts, aged seventeen, and David Stoten, aged twenty-one, who toiled away beside us, drawing and modelling on the bench. Both were already masters of their craft. Stoten, who came to us straight from St Martin's School of Art and holiday jobs on *Mad* magazine, was a gifted draughtsman. He could elongate any face to absolutely ridiculous lengths, horizontally or vertically, and still keep it wholly recognisable. Watts, who came to us by way of the *Leicester Mercury*, on which he had been a schoolboy cartoonist, was just an instinctive caricaturist. Aside from his original creations - like Madonna's singing belly-button, and Manilow as being entirely nose - it was Watts who sussed that our early models were all much too flat. They were suited to the 2-D newspaper past perhaps, but not strongly enough defined for the 3-D televisual future. By sitting at the feet of these infants, Fluck and I learned an inordinate amount.

We originally went to great lengths to achieve the concept of an agreed puppet. Blair was issued with a tiny skull, while Lloyd and Hendra had a tiny bone apiece, which were used to signify everybody's approval of a clay model before it was moulded. This proved a natural seedbed for acrimony and was discontinued, but only after I had demanded reciprocal workshop rights for

7 The two halves of the fibreglass mould in the process of having a core prepared.

8 The finished fibreglass mould, still containing its core, is being prepared by Andy Lee for the foam latex which will make the actual puppet.

9 The foam latex being mixed.

10 Foam latex is injected into the mould to occupy the narrow space between the fibreglass and the core. The injection is made from the rear with a large hypodermic contraption.

approval of the scripts. It was not, however, the end of the basic concept. The model heads would pass up and down between us on the bench as we tried to get the individual handwriting out and the presumed essence of *Spitting Image* in. If we failed to agree, we called in the security guard or the postman. And if he did not find it recognisable and/or funny, we would go back to the drawing board. There was not a huge amount of scope for individual vision. It being television it was the punter's perception, not the the artist's, that ruled.

As the pace quickened to cope with Lloyd's insatiable appetite for heads, the work automatically became more specialised. Very few caricaturists take a great interest in neck, but a good neck is vital to the happiness of a puppeteer. You really could not ask the high-grade child labour to treat this as a high priority problem, so my own working days would be devoted to producing high-speed necks, in much the same way as my father had once laid high-speed bricks. Sadly my father had died shortly before *Spitting Image* was created without realising how close our destinies would become.

Fluck would describe our working life as like being on the assembly line at Fords after being trained to hand-make cars at Rolls-Royce. But it still needed a lot of ingenuity to overcome the fresh problems that kept cropping up, and most of it was supplied by Fluck. Without real problems to solve, Fluck was inclined to regress into the reinvention of useful objects like the wheel, but

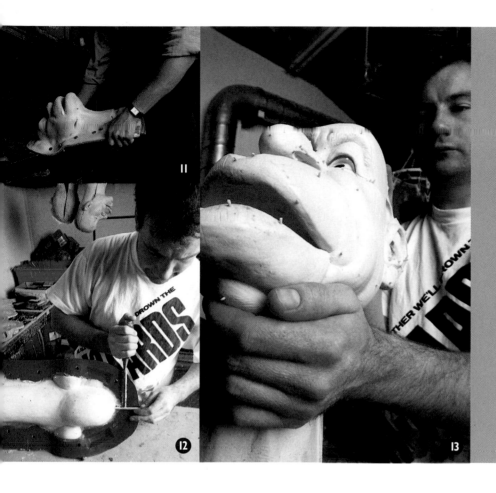

there was no time for such diversions on *Spitting Image*. He went into the series as the esteemed inventor of the eye-movement - a cheap brass and cable arrangement that worked far better than the £800 contraption on offer from the film industry - and came out of it as the hero of numerous other solutions that were both low tech and highly practical. Another Fluck contribution was to scale down the mechanisms behind the bridge of the puppet's nose, which allowed us to get eyes closer together and thus inject a shiftier look. When the puppeteers, angered by the difficulty of keeping their handholds, threatened mutiny, it was Fluck who saved the day again with a visit to the chemists. He thought that fingerstalls at the end of their handgrips might be the answer, and they were. Later we found that these same fingerstalls were excellently suited for the modelling of pitted flesh, which gave greater verisimilitude to characters like General Noriega and Richard Ingrams.

But for all the invention and industry on our part, there was no way that Fluck and I could remotely kid ourselves that we were in control of our own creation. We had come to accept a situation in which we were making funny lookalikes rather than original caricatures, but the acceptance was still painful in the gut. This was not just an old man's complaint. Tim Watts would complain more bitterly than anyone about how the puppeteers would "distort" his own majestic distortions.

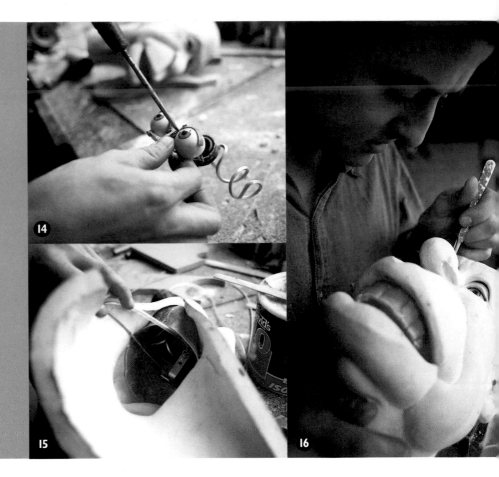

14 The Queen goes to the fitting-up bench, where Guy Stevens is preparing her eyes.

15 Guy attaches the eye movement to a fibreglass skull implanted inside the latex head.

16 The Queen's latex puppet is now fully fitted-up. Guy can be seen giving a final adjustment to the eye mechanism.

We were also fast losing ground outside the workshop. Our original idea was that the show should be almost entirely politics, and they should be as radical as we could manage without being obvious. To this end the Queen was conceived as a sort of benevolent Marxist who had to endure the insufferable woman who happened to be prime minister.

Despite this felicitous invention, it became clear, especially as John Lloyd grew in confidence, that politics was being edged to one side. We had some vigorous debates on this subject in Birmingham, during one of which I was alleged to have tried to strangle him, though I was only feeling the quality of the lapels on his jacket. The truly irritating thing about Lloyd, apart from his talent and charm and blond good looks, was the fact that he was usually right.

The Lloyd argument, in brief, was that politics simply could not sustain the show, especially now that an attempt was being made to make it as snappy as possible. We all knew that when the puppets trotted on the screen, the initial suspension of disbelief was colossal, after which it went very rapidly downhill. This was because they were lousy actors and, being legless, even worse dancers. Aside from popping up and bonking each other on the head, there was nothing they could do of themselves that was intrinsically funny. The only way to disguise their ineptness was to keep the jokes coming thick and fast. The problem was that putting good jokes into the mouths of characters with

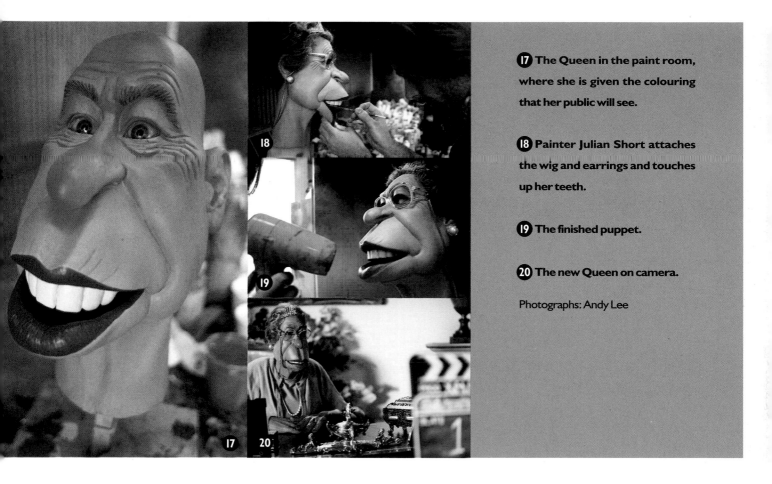

only the most limited range of expression required exceptionally good joke-writers. Writers of this quality were rare, and some of them had no interest in politics whatsoever. But if the show was ever to have a second series it would have to corral these writers and give them scope. And that inevitably meant broadening the show out beyond politics and into the areas of media and entertainment and beyond.

We reluctantly bought the argument as far as entertainment figures were concerned, but when requests for sports stars started coming down, the workshop played merry hell. This, it was argued, was like being asked to caricature people for no better reason than that they were there. But somehow Steve "Very Interesting" Davis and a few others managed to squeeze through the manufacturing process over my live, quivering body. Then I met up with my old patron Peter Cook, after an intermission of twenty-three years, who told me that the thing he most liked about *Spitting Image* was the way it sent up the sports stars.

There was a lot of luck involved in whether a caricature worked well as a puppet. It helped if a character had a big mouth, as this made it much easier for the puppeteer to do his or her job. The Queen's puppet benefited enormously from being based on a caricature with a big mouth, as did the Walter Matthau and Bernard Levin puppets. A consequence of Mrs Thatcher's having a small, tight mouth was that her puppet was always very difficult to manipulate. Since we could not take the liberty of dispensing big mouths to all and sundry, it just became a discomfort we all had to live with.

There were, however, certain areas in which we were prepared to adjust reality. It has been said that time is the best caricaturist, but this is not always the case. In her old films, Lauren Bacall really did have extraordinary cat's eyes, ones that turned sharply up, but by the time Tim Watts got round to modelling her they had turned the other way. With characters like Bacall, and to some extent Laurence Olivier, we would compromise the caricature to include a large element of how people remembered they looked, rather than how they actually do look, for the sake of credibility on the screen.

It might be thought that after so many compromises of our political and aesthetic outlook, Fluck and I should have lost all stomach with the show. "What on earth are we doing here?" did become a kind of catchphrase of the partnership but on my side it was a joke and it usually, though not invariably, was with Fluck. Despite all the disappointments, there was always the sense of participating in something quite extraordinary. It might not be the acme of caricature or the most hard-edged political satire but it still seemed like a creation worth persevering with. And many of our conflicts had not been so much over principle, as coming to an understanding of what the creation could do, and what it couldn't.

The benefits of actually knowing what we were doing were almost immediately apparent in the second series, in which we achieved a rough balance of fifty per cent political material to fifty per cent media, entertainment and sport. This gave the front-line writers the range they wanted to aim at, though

in practice they tended to specialise. Ian Hislop and Nick Newman from *Private Eye* provided the sharp political stuff while Rob Grant and Doug Naylor, who would later go on to fashion *Red Dwarf*, provided what became one of *Spitting Image's* richest ingredients - silliness. My personal favourite *Spitting Image* sketch of all time was a Grant-Naylor conception involving the Gielgud and Olivier puppets contemplating old acquaintances, all "gone, goney, gone".

There was a certain amount of objective evidence that other people were also coming to appreciate the improvement. The first series struggled to achieve an audience of 6.5 million, while the second averaged 10.5 million, peaking at 11.4 million for the show which first featured a caricature of the Queen Mother. However, we did tend to discount the last figure as that particular show had been hugely over-promoted in the *Daily Express* which instructed all its readers to switch off as a protest against "squalid backroom boys who hide snide and shallow jokes behind their sniggering puppet face".

That aside, the press could not have been more fawning. The popular newspapers would be forever ringing up asking to use our puppets to illustrate their articles, while the critical columns in the quality papers - apart from the *Guardian*, which preserved its distrust - became complimentary to an almost embarrassing degree. We would eventually become the critics' choice as the best light entertainment programme of the year.

These accolades made it possible for people to enjoy the show's first Christmas party even after sinking their teeth into mince pies secretly whipped up from the foam debris of redundant characters. Of the higher command, only the watchful Fluck spotted the pies for what they were - the revenge of the child labour. Offered his pie, Fluck politely inquired, "Anyone I know?"

The current *Spitting Image* title sequence was designed, made and shot by David Stoten. As can be seen it harks back, in a forward-looking way, to the era of Punch and Judy. It also harks back to the era of glove puppets in *Spitting Image* which first flowered, decayed and died before the original pilot programme. The glove puppets on display here are of Gadaffi, Gorbachev, John Major and President Bush. The business of recycling bits of the past in order to create an impact on the present has always been one of *Spitting Image's* central strategies. How long can it last?

Deadly Sins at Rainbow's End

Chapter 11 When Spitting Image started to achieve some success there were those on the Left who saw it heralding the last days of Mrs Thatcher, just as TW3 and the early 1960s satire boom signposted the end of the Macmillan era. They proved to be some last days. In fact, we only managed to topple her after six, long, gruelling years and then only with more than a little help from her old chums in the Tory Party.

Pablo Bach, Janice Tchalenko and I survey unglazed work in progress on the Seven Deadly Sins project wearing essential protective equipment.
Photograph: Howard Gray

Spitting Image never did manage to achieve the political cutting edge that Fluck and I had originally always seen as part of its purpose. The reason for this did not reside in any notion of a need for "balance" on television. A much more important factor was the eternal quest for characters who would make the show work. This automatically meant that none of the leading politicians in Opposition could be left unmolested. Mrs Thatcher and the crazed Michael Heseltine were probably the two most popular political characters in the show for many years, but they were very closely followed by Neil Kinnock as Kinnochio, Hattersley as a spitting machine, and David Steel as a babe cradled in the arms of a satanic David Owen.

We were also surprised at the degree to which caricature combined with puppetry proved not so much savage as endearing. Politicians were often discomforted by their puppet images, but they did represent membership of a weird kind of popular elect. It was probably more discomforting for them when their images ceased to appear.

Another thing that militated against a consistent radical line was the fact that the show was made with the direct input of literally scores of people - ranging from devout monarchists to hard-line Marxists - who would be quite unable to agree the political time of day among themselves. It's also possible that I was more of a traditionalist than I originally gave myself credit for. I had some inkling of this when my son Shem borrowed my suit to go for his first big job interview. The consequence was that the same suit worked at the *Observer* again after an interval of twenty-two years. In some obscure, ancestral way I found this deeply pleasing.

While the show's insights may be too diffuse to have any decisive effect on how people vote, I think that it undoubtedly has influenced perceptions. I noticed this in my own case after Mrs Thatcher's triumph in the 1987 Election. I was leafing through a set of photographs of the new Tory Cabinet in one of the Sunday newspapers, and I asked Deirdre if she had seen them. She replied, "That's not photographs of them you idiot, they're photographs of your *Spitting Image* puppets." And over the years, I've noticed with delight that many other people have acquired the tendency to confuse the caricature with the real person. Considering the large sums of money spent on PR by famous people to induce a heightened appreciation of themselves, this is no small achievement and probably has helped to create a healthier disrespect for those in high places. I would say that our modest, but continuing, political effect has been to keep the feet of the nation's leaders just that little bit closer to the ground. It's probably among the reasons why *Spitting Image* has proved to be rather more than a flash in the pan.

The Spitting Image company is now in its tenth year, and in the process of producing its fourteenth series, without any sign of flagging. There have been changes, of course, of which the most obvious, but least important, has been location. Drummed out of dockland by the onward march of the Canary Wharf development back in more cheerful days for the property market, we were able to regroup quite contentedly in Aldgate, less than two miles away.

Of the original Gang of Five only Fluck and myself survive as major shareholders in the company. Hendra reverted to his original role as a satirist in the United States, Jon Blair set up his own production company, while John Lloyd took off on other pursuits that would add to his appallingly large collection of BAFTA awards before moving on to make some of the best commercials seen on British television. Even Fluck and I have ceased to be hands-on in the old sense. Fluck's main energies are now engaged outside Spitting Image in the areas of robotics and environmental sculptures, which speak unto and are moved by the wind, rain and sun.

My main contribution to Spitting Image now, aside from some original drawing, is keeping the show on the road as chairman of the enterprise. This evolution from irresponsible anarchist to fat capitalist has been hugely assisted by Joanna Beresford, the company's managing director, and by Richard Bennett, the accountant. We work together as a thoroughly modern management team. When Bennett and I came back from Moscow recently, flourish-

The management of *Spitting Image* has always believed there is more to life than showbiz. There is also merchandising, for example. Opposite: "The Chicken Song" , a spin-off from the show and a number one hit record. Above: a tuna fish, man-made for the advertising industry.
Photographs: above, Andy Lee; opposite, Terry Beddis

ing a scrap of paper that showed that we only had to train up the Russians to do their own show to be on a piece of the action, Joanna was among the first to congratulate us on "coming back with twenty-five per cent of nothing".

The other major personnel change has been in the puppets. We went into that fraught first series with a couple of understrength platoons of around fifty puppets. Now we have an army, 800 strong, to meet the requirements of our series in the spring and autumn. Even allowing time for pre-production work, this still leaves us over half the year to do other things. Some of these other things, it must be confessed, are more popular with the workers than the actual show.

One of the first Spitting Image diversifications, other than Mrs Thatcher rubber chews for dogs, was into publishing. We currently have three Spitting Image books waiting to be launched and of the five we did in the past, three were best-sellers. Another one was Luck and Flaw's *Treasure Island*, which finally found its one, true publisher in Faber and Faber. The early volumes contained some memorable images, of which the most potent was a centrefold of a Prince Andrew nude lookalike on silk sheets with four pounds of Cumberland sausages in its lap. Among the recent crop, the most striking is perhaps the

"The Last Supper", with Mrs Thatcher in the chair, was prepared for "Cutting Edge", an exhibition of satirical works staged at the Barbican in 1992. Other characters from left to right: Norman Lamont, Kenneth Clarke, David Mellor, Douglas Hurd, John Major, Virginia Bottomley, the head of Neil Kinnock (on platter), Nigel Lawson, Cecil Parkinson, Geoffrey Howe, Norman Tebbit,

Michael Heseltine, Christopher Patten. Under the table: Denis Thatcher. The spread won unusually favourable comment in the press, partly because of its attention to fine details like the "Water into Wine List" and the itemised bill which logged the consumption of five loaves, two fishes and thirty-four lagers.
Art direction: Alex Evans and Andrew de Emmony
Photograph: Greg Pullen

Rupert Murdoch lookalike as a page-seven hunk wielding its willie which, on closer inspection, is a rather limp-looking character resembling Andrew Neil. Books, we found, were very popular with the workshop as they gave greater scope for individual creativity than was possible when the show was running. Publishing, therefore, became part of our child labour retention policy.

We could not keep them all. Tim Watts irresponsibly got himself properly educated at art school and now sits at the right hand of the film animator Dick Williams. But we did get to keep quite a few. David Stoten is now our expert on stop-motion while still working as a caricaturist alongside Pablo Bach, a brilliant Argentinean who joined during the second series. Stephen Bendelack, who originally mucked out the chapel for us, is now a director of *Spitting Image* and greatly in demand as a creator of title sequences for other shows. Andy de Emmony, who once painted puppet heads, also directs *Spitting Image* and is both director and script editor of a new children's programme called *Cave-In*. Scott Brooker, who ran the eye-fitting department, is now the company expert on new character creation, which has been the clue to the other main diversifications, into new shows and advertising.

Cover story. The hand of our photographer, above left, John Lawrence Jones hovers expertly over one of his elaborate, puppet-shooting arrangements. He is shooting the puppet Gielgud for the back cover of *The Appallingly Disrespectful Spitting Image Book*. It came out so well that we decided to have two front covers - Gielgud as one, with Norman Tebbit, seen right awaiting a model limb, as the other. We discovered later that some eager fans bought the book twice. This was not intended.

Photographs: John Lawrence Jones
Book design: Alex Evans

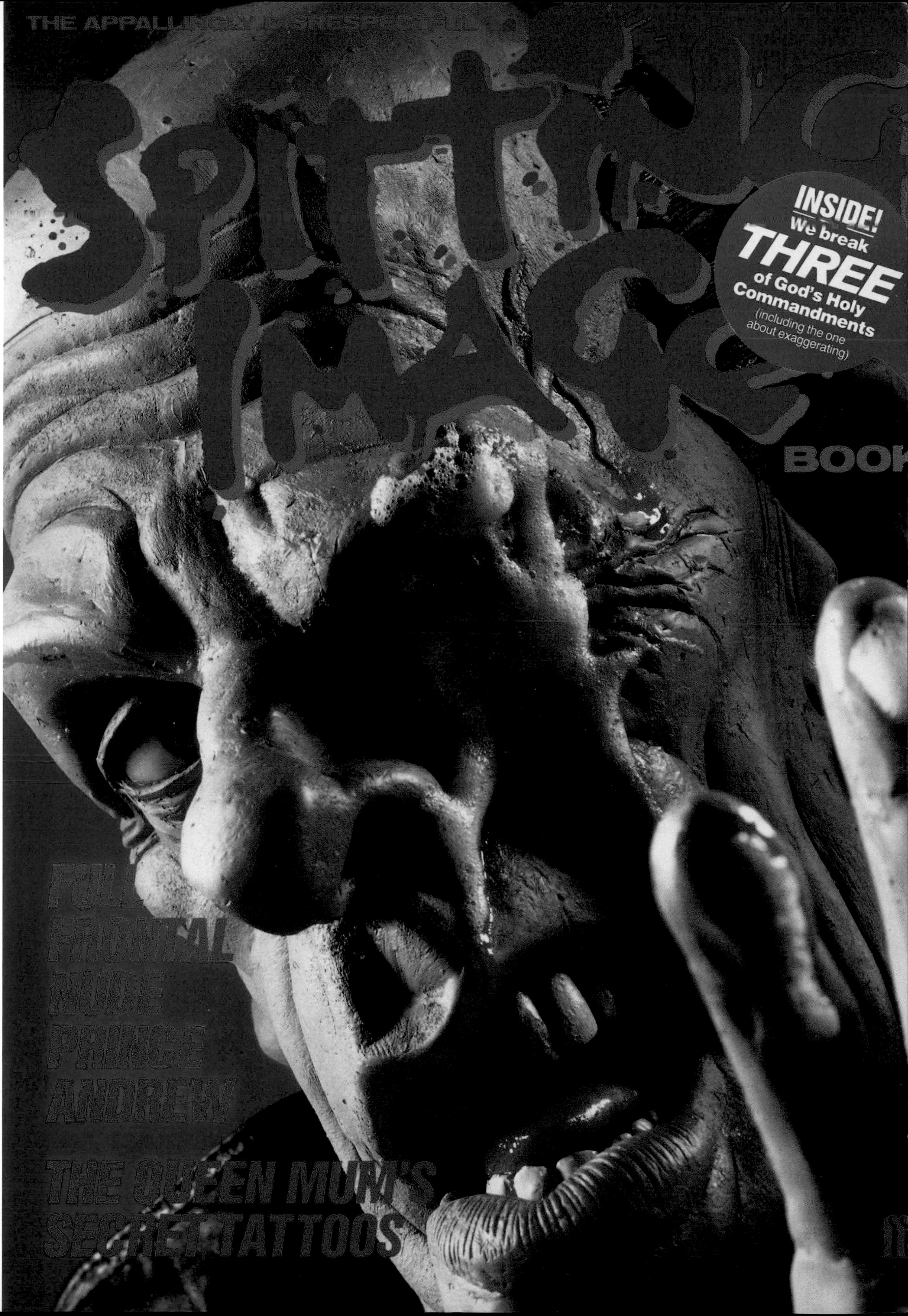

THE APPALLINGLY DISRESPECTFUL
SPITTING IMAGE
BOOK
INSIDE! We break THREE of God's Holy Commandments (including the one about exaggerating)
FULL FRONTAL NUDE PRINCE ANDREW
THE QUEEN MUM'S SECRET TATTOOS

This image of Prince Andrew, as a highly eligible bachelor, first appeared in *The Appallingly Disrespectful Spitting Image Book*. Entitled "Hot Dog", its wholly flattering caption read: "Andy is by far the dishiest Royal, not having inherited many of the genetic disorders which mar the royal bloodline. Not for him the hump of Richard III, nor the babbling insanity of Canute, but rather the legendary genitalia of Cuthbert the Ploughman (815-820) who, according to legend, left a small furrow "wherever he strode".

I would not say that this image sold the book, but it certainly earned it some attention as it was widely denounced for having a tasteless quality. Curiously enough this was not a factor that disturbed us while making the model. Our main concern was whether it was funny. I remember describing the basic idea to Rob Grant and Doug Naylor, our two main scriptwriters, and they were not over-impressed. But when they saw the model, they fell about.

The making of Prince Andrew was very much a group workshop effort, though special effort must be accorded to Peter Fluck who fashioned the lean, hard body in plasticine. The sausages were from Cumberland and, as it happens, rather tasty.

Photograph: John Lawrence Jones

When Prince Andrew and Sarah Ferguson were married in 1986 we had no problem assembling a Buckingham Palace balcony scene for the new Duke and Duchess of York. Produced for publicity purposes, the photograph, above, consists entirely of characters we had previously made for *Spitting Image*. Above right: we also updated James Gillray's portrayal of an earlier Duke and Duchess in 1792 but, unlike his effort, ours was not published.

Photographs: above right, John Lawrence Jones; above, Stephen Bendelack

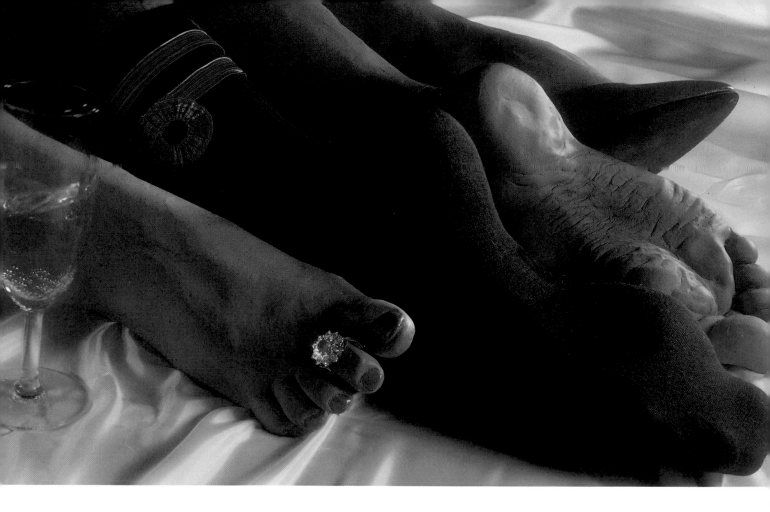

FASHIONABLE CONTRASTS; or — The Duchess's little Shoe yielding to the Magnitude of the Duke's Foot.

Far left: Princess Diana and Princess Anne, who were alleged to have had some differences, appeared nose-to-nose in one of our early books.

Left: There was resistance, even within *Spitting Image*, to caricaturing the Queen Mother, but it seemed unfair to leave her out. This appearance was made in *The Appallingly Disrespectful Spitting Image Book*.

Photographs: John Lawrence Jones

These are characters who appeared in the television show, but who were all given a little extra grooming for display in our book *Spitting Images*. Above: Neil Kinnock as Kinnochio with Glenys, as Jiminy Cricket, being a guide to the Labour leader's conscience. Far right: Jack Nicholson, bursting with rude health. Right: Mike Tyson, the heavyweight boxing champion, with whom Tim Watts achieved his ambition to model a character wholly from the back. The significance of the pigeon is that Tyson kept pigeons on his tenement roof when he was a young boy. Fistic folklore has it that he discovered the more lethal qualities in his make-up when he found somebody messing with his birds.

Photographs: John Lawrence Jones

Absolutely NO GIMMICKS except for the Free Poster inside

Contains the Celebrity Mega Mix of The Chicken Song

(Frank Sinatra, Dolly Parton, Bruce Springsteen, Cilla Black, Bob Dylan and Tina Turner join in their all time

The *Spit in your Ear* album was the delicate come-on to Spitting Image's first LP featuring songs from the show and some that had been specially composed for this release. Some were sung by an in-house royal pop group called The Nobs.

The numbers included "Uranus", "Clean Rugby Songs", "I've never met a nice South African" and "Botha Tells the Truth".

Photograph: John Lawrence Jones
Design: Alex Evans

The *Spitting Image Komic Book* gave the workshop the opportunity to run amok in cartoon form. The cover, left, was conceived by David Stoten, while Tim Watts supplied a series of powerful insights into the loneliness of Dr David Owen (example above). There were also diagrams to indicate where a sumo wrestler placed his testicles. It was all quite unbelievably silly.

Drawing: David Stoten

Design: Alex Evans

Overleaf: Mrs Thatcher, right, as she appeared in our book *Spitting Images* and, left, how she would have appeared on the cover of *Thatcha: Ten Years of the Dragon* if we had got around to finishing the book.

Photographs: left, Andy de Emmony; right, John Lawrence Jones

Design: Alex Evans

SPITTING IMAGE

THATCHA!

TEN YEARS OF THE DRAGON

...and on, and on, and on, and on

MAGGIE'S ELECTION HAT-TRICK
How she talks through it and still gets voted in!

THE FALKLANDS WAR
How she responded when the ships were down

GREAT BRITISH SELL-OFFS
Telecom, gas, electricity, water. Everything must go . . . up in price!

THE OFFICIAL SECRETS ACT
20
things you'll never know!
(no story inside)

Not General Galtieri

Pablo Bach, seen working on the model for a Thatcher Toby Jug, is now Spitting Image's head caricaturist. To mark his elevation to this high office he donned beret and chocker, waxed his moustache and bandaged his vital modelling digits.

Bach first joined Spitting Image in 1986 at the age of twenty-four. Over the years he has drawn and modelled just about everybody claiming to be anybody. Opposite: his Mrs Thatcher, tucking into Great Britain, Winston Churchill and Griff Rhys Jones. Left: Saddam Hussein.

Above left: a plaster bust of the sculptor Sir Eduardo Paolozzi, who incautiously presented Bach with a sculpted dragon, and received this in return.

Bach claims to have learned modelling skills on his grandmother's knee, but he later refined them at the National College of Arts in Buenos Aires. We used to have to persuade the immigration authorities every year that Bach, among the most liberal of men, was not General Galtieri in disguise. Then Bach fashioned a gargoyle for an extension to a Cambridge college, and was photographed chumming up with Prince Philip at the opening. Since then, there has been no problem.

Behind the scenes of the "I can't believe it's not butter" advertisements. Top: the two Scott Brooker creations as they appear on the screen. Above: a studio in Shepperton where a team of puppeteers animate the cows for the camera.

he advertising breakthrough has been the most intriguing one for me. In the days when Luck and Flaw was vainly trying to sell out to the advertising world, we came to feel that caricature and advertising had to be essentially antipathetic - the former being largely negative in conception (i.e. against something or somebody), while the latter had to be positive. There were probably also some subsidiary negative factors that held us back. We would, for example, rather lose an account than a jest. I remember one time we spent over an hour kicking our heels in the waiting room of some advertising mogul in the West End. The main feature of this room was that it was absolutely festooned with glass cases containing "Golden Arrows", one of the highest accolades in the advertising world. When our award-winning man deigned to come out and see us, Fluck said in a conversational way, "I never knew that you were so remarkably fond of archery."

Looking back, I realise that our mistake was to assume that our advertising had to be about stunting up special effects of the benighted chameleon and rainbow variety. What we should have been looking for was some way to fuse the positive and negative elements. Later we found it could be done, but only

with humour. This simple discovery took us an awful long time to make, but it's the reason why margarine advertisements are more amusing these days.

The importance of Scott Brooker to this, and other, enterprises is that he creates characters that are not just distortions of famous people. The skill grew out of an aspect of his early work on the show, which was creating subsidiary puppets by cannibalising spare parts from redundant heads. The wildebeest, the white cat and the two squirrels having it off in the corner of the screen would be Brooker manufactures. More recently his characters have starred in productions like *Green Gilbert, Round the Bend* (produced by Hat Trick), and *The Wingein' Pom*.

Spitting Image, like every other independent production company in television, has to be ready for just about anything in the future. We have broadened our range, even to the extent of producing shows like *The Mary Whitehouse Experience* and *Beethoven's Not Dead* that have no animation content at all, but it is still inescapably a labour-intensive operation in an industry where good deals are increasingly hard to find. One of the main reasons for the popularity of advertising work with ourselves, and with people of the calibre of John Lloyd, is because it is one of the few areas in broadcasting where you can get enough money to play and experiment with new ideas. This is fun for us,

"Grizzly" Bear, top, is the star of a new children's show called *Cave-In*. Made for Carlton TV, it is the creation of Andrew de Emmony, above, who started his working life on *Spitting Image* as a puppet-painter before moving on to higher things.
Photograph: Greg Pullen

Theatrical venture. The flames emerging from Pablo Bach's model, above, are real, though the image represents the marriage of two transparencies - one of the dragon belching gas-lit fire against a black velvet backdrop, the other of a hunk of black-painted metal with gas jets ablaze behind the carved out lettering. It was created as a poster for *Dragon*, a new English version of Yevgeny Shvats' play, recently produced at the National Theatre.

Photograph: Stephen Bendelack

Studies in power. Leaders of the main political parties, right, done for a *Private Eye* 1992 General Election poster.

Photograph: John Lawrence Jones

but hardly a good comment on the industry as a whole.

While nobody can predict the shape of British television by the end of the century, the current trends are not encouraging. The consumerist fragmentation that afflicted the press through the 1980s is now all too evident in television, making it harder to take on large, imaginative projects. We already know that the marriage of new technology with untrammelled commercialism is an excellent one for breeding more media. However, its capacity for producing quality and more real choice is well short of being proved. It may not be so very long before Bruce Springsteen's analysis of American television - "57 channels and nothin' on" - applies equally well to our own visual media.

I have no vested interest in carping at American TV, particularly as Spitting Image has sold one custom-built series to the NBC network and is in the process of selling another to CBS, but overall it seems to provide a model for the future that we would do very well to avoid.

Spitting Image's own future depends to a large degree on how the industry evolves and, to some extent, on its own capacity to develop in interesting ways. The show has changed quite significantly. Because of our improved studio and workshop techniques we can, when the occasion demands, shoot almost half the programme on the day before transmission. This means that we can be much more topical than in the past. Even so, it is probably true to say that the show has not changed so much as the people who watch it.

Lord of the jungle

Above: Scott Brooker, pictured with furry friends in the cab of the *Wingein' Pom* **van, is Spitting Image's foremost creator of original puppets. His characters provide background figures to the human lookalikes on** *Spitting Image,* **but they are the stars of other company productions like** *Green Gilbert* **and** *Wingein' Pom.* **His two crows, Ronnie and**

Reggie, made for *Wingein' Pom* were a sensation on French television where, redubbed as two Marseilles gangsters, they ran for eternity. Above: working drawings for some of his animal characters and a demonstration of his hidden, but still bouyant, talent for representing human character. The figure on the right is Dragon One, a character sketch made for the National Theatre in preparation for staging Yevgeny Shvats' play *Dragon*.
Photograph: Nick Lockett

Man for the medium

Stephen Bendelack, right, seen directing *Spitting Image* on set, was our first employee. We hired him fresh out of art school to muck out the chapel and run errands while we were sweating over the *Spitting Image* prototypes. He was an inquisitive sort of cove who made a point of knowing everything about television and everybody in it, which saved us no end of money on reference books. He now directs comedy videos, a number of television shows, and has developed a specialised line in title sequences. The storyboard, above, illustrates his title sequence for the Spitting Image production, *The Mary Whitehouse Experience*, an unusual venture for us in that it has no animation content. Like other independent television compa-

THE MARY WHITEHOUSE EXPERIENCE
SCRIPT
SKETCH NO. 98
DRAFT A DELETE

nies, Spitting Image is involved in a tough struggle for survival, and diversification outside puppetry is one way of hedging our bets. Keeping Bendelack on the books, with enough funds for a very occasional haircut, is also a way of ensuring that the bets are placed correctly.

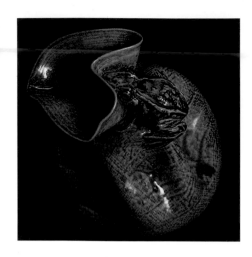

Above: a complete sin. Avarice, the first of our Seven Deadly Sins to reach a salt-glazed condition, features a toad at the throat of a mediaeval money bag.
Below: Cilla Black and Norman Lamont as panto dames, done for Liberty's Christmas shop windows.
Photographs: Greg Pullen

John Lloyd, who has the grace to tell a story against himself every now and then, once told me of a lecture he gave to a group of students, comparing and contrasting the slickness and efficiency of a third series show under his unified command with our bumbling, conflict-ridden effort in the first show featuring the much-derided Exchequers sit-com about a rest home for former prime ministers. By way of illustration he screened both the shows. Both were appreciated, but it was Exchequers that really had them falling off their seats.

It's possible to see now that the early shows did not suffer so much from poor scripts, which was originally thought to be the case, so much as from utterly distracting characters. It was only when these figures ceased to be startling, by viewers becoming accustomed to them, that the words had a serious glimmer of chance.

John Lloyd would begin to exploit their ability to crack more than one-liners but it would be Bill Dare, the show's current producer, who felt confident enough to allow them to be something more than relentless joke-machines. On the occasions when Mrs Thatcher and Neil Kinnock fell off their political perches, Bill Dare even managed to get the puppets to express pathos. In the beginning nobody, would have thought that was possible.

The other intriguing awareness that dawned on us is that there is an iconography of famous heads that we all carry around with us. It is the main reason why it is so hard to caricature people who are not famous - they might have the head but they do not have the iconography. This may tie in with recent medical research which suggests that babies recognise their mothers not through discerning their features, but through an awareness of the shape of their mother's heads. A mother, after all, is usually a baby's most famous person.

We increasingly found that the measure of a successful caricature is its fidelity to the iconography rather than the actual head. This is why the "roughing out" stage - making the bold shape - ranks at least equal in importance to all the telling little disfigurements. Thus we are most satisfied with John Major as Prime Minister because we feel that we have got the unusual iconography of his unusual head exactly right. He is also highly esteemed for his ability to use up our surplus supplies of grey emulsion preservative.

My own head is largely preserved by the work I do in ceramics, which has yet to become a money-making activity, but you never know. Currently I am collaborating with the ceramicist Janice Tchalenko and Pablo Bach on a series of pieces illustrating the Seven Deadly Sins. We are making excellent progress with six of the sins though we may require a fourth, and much younger, collaborator to help out with Lust.

It will be apparent to anybody who has read this far that I am one of those people who cannot cross the road without the collaboration of a travelling companion. This probably disqualifies me from the title of artist, but I do get through a reasonable amount of work with a little help from my friends.

Work in progress. Above: the bench occupied by Pablo Bach and myself, when escaping the burdens of high office. Working drawings for Anger and Pride are pinned to the wall; most of the pot-bellied objects on the bench are Pavarottis. Left: caricature sketch of a "Thatchers" Toby Jug with Denis as its handle. The jug was made to commemorate ten years of Tory rule.

Photograph: Howard Gray

Back to nature: models of the Duchess of York, above left, and John Bryan, above right. Right: Rupert Murdoch, media emperor.

Photographs: Greg Pullen

STOP
PRESS

Index

Acknowledgements

In remembering my own life I came to depend heavily on the prompting of many other people, starting with four generations of my own family. I am most indebted to my mother, **Winifred,** and my wife, **Deirdre Amsden,** but I cannot think of anybody who seriously held back. Indeed, they all seemed particularly good at recalling episodes that I hoped had long since been forgotten. I thank them for all their memories, pleasant and painful.

Outside my family, I was greatly assisted by **Peter Jones,** Spitting Image's resourceful PR representative, who, at my behest, ruthlessly interrogated some of the people who have known me better than most. They included **John Lloyd, David King, Paul Hogarth, Pat Gavin** and, most especially, **Peter Fluck** and his wife **Anne de Bruyne,** all of whom gave most generously of their time. I am also most grateful to **Steve Haines, John Kelly, John Lawrence Jones, Lyn Owen, Michael Rand** and **Tim Watts** for the help they gave in the preparation of this book.

Once I had assembled a heap of all I knew and all I could find of my life and work, I called in two friends, **Lewis Chester** and **Alex Evans,** to help me put it into shape. Miraculously, they still remain my friends.

At Spitting Image, I am most beholden to **Joanna Beresford** and **Richard Bennett** for shouldering my administrative cares, and to **Angela Sheahan** for supplying my absent mind when there was still contemporary work to be done. The other characters at Spitting Image who kept the show on the road while the boss was intently scrutinising his own navel were: **Pablo Bach, Stephen Bendelack, Scott Brooker, Anne Cartwright, Rebecca Cotterill, Andrew de Emmony, Henry Guiste, Nicky Herbert, Andy Lee, Neal Palmer, Guy Stevens, Kate Stirling** and **David Stoten.**

I sincerely thank them all.